— CONTENTS —

Introduction

It is over 20 years since I started gathering material on the erstwhile Didcot, Newbury & Southampton Railway. That it is a favourite is beyond doubt, a fondness I know I share with many, particularly in the local area. Having also been involved in the presentation of four books appertaining to the route already, I would have thought the appetite would have been well and truly satisfied, but it appears not and I am regularly asked if there is anything new or pending. Hence the appearance then of this small work.

My known interest in the DNS has also resulted in the acquisition of new facts and photographs on a fairly regular basis, who knows perhaps what may still be waiting to be discovered - I am still looking! The text and photographs of the present work are intended however, to stand alone from other works and as such there must of necessity be some small duplication in order to permit of completeness. Otherwise I hope the reader will find the new information and photographs of interest - I know I could hardly contain myself when I came upon the cover view by chance at an antiques fair for just a few pence. Other finds too have been a fascinating voyage of discovery, that appertaining to Mr. Knutton, the Winchester Station Master a classic example. Notwithstanding the above, I should also state I maintain an interest in other lines, areas, and companies, the railway map does not start and end on the DNS even if my regular journeys to Winchester and on the A34 do mean there is often more than a wistful longing to once more see a train in that particular landscape.

Acknowledgements

The production of this book is a combination of material gathered over the years from a number of sources, and aside from the photographic credits given in the text, I would like to thank Ian Coulson, David Postle at the Kidderminster Railway Museum - well worth a visit, Roger Simmonds, Peter Squibb and friends within the Signalling Record Society. Without their support and encouragement much of what is recorded here would have remained hidden away from gaze. I hope you agree it does deserve a wider audience.

WINCHESTER

(Great Western)
...a snapshot in time...

Kevin Robertson

KRB Publications

ISBN 0-9542035-1-8

Published by
KRB Publications
2 Denewulf Close
BISHOPS WALTHAM
Hants
SO32 1GZ

Printed by M & S Print, Hailsham (01323) 449477

Chapter One

THE EARLY YEARS

It was wet on 4th May 1885 or to be more exact it was more like a day of almost continuous rain. An unfortunate beginning to what was meant to be an auspicious occasion - the arrival of and opening of the new railway between Newbury and Winchester.

Despite the outward show of pomp and festivities however, this was really little more than an announcement of hoped for grandiose things to come. The railway from Newbury having arrived at Winchester and formed a dead-end, stopping abruptly in a field at Bar End just south of the passenger station, and still some twelve miles short of its avowed destination at Southampton.

Indeed that town was within the title of the little company itself, the Didcot, Newbury and Southampton Railway and whose first section of line from Didcot as far as Newbury had opened for business some three years earlier in 1882, and after which all efforts had been concentrated on forming an independent link to the south coast, and contrary to the original prospectus of a connection with the existing London & South Western near Micheldever. (The story of the erstwhile early years, the twists and turns of fate and subsequent hopes and failures of the DNS company proper is described fully in the Didcot, Newbury & Southampton Railway, by Paul Karau, Mike Parsons and Kevin Robertson, and published by Wild Swan.)

This then was a difficult start to Winchester's new railway. The little DNS had been in no position to operate the new route themselves and so an agreement was entered into with the mighty Great Western for this purpose. As such the GWR could effectively 'call-the-tune', and this they did in many ways, at times often seemingly pedantic in the extreme and no more so than their requirements prior to the opening. A number of these issues relate to locations other than Winchester and so are out of place in this narrative, but even at Winchester minor matters seemed set to delay proceedings, including such a trivial item as the GWR's reference to no knob or knocker being attached to the door of the Station Master's house! More obvious and relevant omissions at Winchester were recorded in a report from early 1885 and which commented, "Everything is in a very backward state. The Goods Shed is not complete, the sidings are not in, the extensive goods yard requires ballasting and the passenger station buildings and yard are very incomplete.......the line requires a great deal of ballast between Winchester Station and Sutton Scotney........the platforms should be paved the length of the buildings. The telegraph posts are all up, but the wires are not yet put up between Whitchurch and Winchester. Clocks are required at all the stations and signal boxes......". In truth much of this work would have been completed anyway, although it appears there was in some respects little in the way of urgency displayed. T.B. Sands - and who completed the very first brief history of the DNS over 30 years ago, (Published by Oakwood Press in 1971 and now long out of print), is of the opinion that the date of opening had originally been set for 24 March 1885, but that this was delayed. '....due to the inability of the GWR to find sufficient staff.' This may well have been the case as the requisite Board of Trade inspection had previously taken place on 21 March and it was to be a further six weeks before the formal opening and public services would commence.

Opposite; - Construction at Winchester in either the summer of 1883 or 1884-the latter is most likely. The photograph is taken looking south from where the footbridge to St. Giles Hill later crossed the railway, this may explain the apparent brief piece of what could just be scaffold visible at lower left. In the distance is the timber staging for what would be East Hill bridge. It is also just possible to discern the distinct tree pattern that adourned the top of St. Catherine's Hill. Perusal of the land Terriers shows the amount of land purchased by the railway at this point and which includes a sizeable extra width due to the depth of the cutting. Contemporary reports indicate that the excavated material was tipped onto Winnall Moors and so meaning the tunnel, which would have been behind the photographer, was complete and full wagons could be drawn back and replaced. Later much material was also excavated from the right hand side and which considerably reduced the cutting height compared with the right. With East Hill Bridge complete, excavated material was used to form the site of Bar end yard. Upwards of 35 men can be seen at work, although the necessity of using a time exposure has resulted in several ghost images - somewhat appropriate over a century later. The wagons are typical contractors vehicles and would have been placed by a steam engine. Notice there is no sign of horse-power being employed, possibly the men are engaged in 'shaping off', the main excavation having been carried out by 'steam navvy'.

Hampshire County Museum Service

At long last and after a quarter of a century of searching the elusive one turns up! It was always known that photographs had been taken of the opening day but it was not sure if they had survived-witness what appear to be photographers also on the wall opposite the station. The newness of the chalk is a most noticeable feature against which the dark station building appears largely complete although it has yet to receive its decorative ironwork on the turrets. Brickwork for the building may have come from Hermitage, north of Newbury, although this is for the moment not confirmed. In time for the opening the necessary furniture was provided at Winchester and the other stations south of Newbury by the GWR at a cost of £372 1s 1d, although just three months later an additional £12 6s 9d was necessary. In the photograph, flags are seen bedecking the canopy, tunnel mouth and signal box whilst there is a multitude of people not only on the station approach but also on the path above the tunnel. Near the latter is the DNS style Station Master's house. The train has arrived at what was later the 'up' side, the down platform complete but not in use. At the north end of the building it is just possible to discern the original water tank, reported as supported on timber legs and which was only present for a very short time. There is also only a single starting signal - that at the end of what was later the 'down' platform was not provided until at least 1893. The sharp curve of the train as it appears in the tunnel is accounted for the single line of rails only after that point, even though the earthworks, including the tunnel were built to accommodate a double line. The track in the down platform would also appear to be of the 'inside-keyed' type. Unfortunately the locomotive(s) at the head of the train is not reported, whilst contemporary reports indicate the train itself consisted of four first class carriages, twelve first/second class composite vehicles, three brake vans and a saloon-not necessarily in that precise order. Study of the original print reveals the nearest vehicle to be a bogie 3rd, to Diagram D4, Lot No 431, and almost new at the time. Its running number was in the series 1723-1752. There then follow four 2nd / 3rd. class vehicles and what may well be a Brake 3rd. to Diagram 20 and having four compartments - two either side of a central guards compartment. After this is a four compartment first although it is not known if this was four or six wheeled stock. The remainder of the train is indistinguishable. On all the coaches oil lighting is used and there are footboards commensurate with the period. Those vehicles most recently outshopped can be identified by the lighter coloured roofs. (On the day the first train comprising the vehicles referred to above, left Winchester carrying invited guests and proceeded to Newbury. There is was boarded by further invited guests and augmented also by four additional vehicles - details of which are not known, and a second locomotive. It then returned to Winchester for the opening ceremony. What is not certain is at what stage in the day the photograph was taken.)

Hampshire County Museum Service

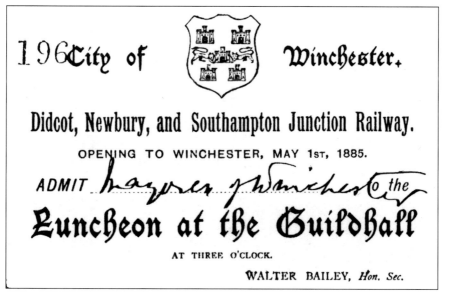

Suffice to say then that as far as Winchester was concerned on that wet May day, many among the assembled throng no doubt wished the line would soon be completed through to Southampton, and especially those who had invested in the venture. Publicly, the work so far completed in the area of Hill Lane and The Polygon areas of Southampton was for the moment 'temporarily suspended, and it was hoped would be re-started as soon as possible.

For the moment though that appeared as if it could only be some way distant, as the independent DNS Company had used both all of its available share capital and borrowing facilities. Any further attempt at raising additional capital would run a considerable risk of over-capitalisation. But all this was behind the outward facade of that days celebrations, whilst in appearance the new railway could have been mistaken for being under both the operation and ownership of the Great Western - the station at Winchester very much in contemporary GWR style. One exception was in the form of the standard DNS type cottage perched high above the station almost atop the tunnel mouth. Elsewhere on the route this design was used almost exclusively to form part of the station buildings and accommodation, but here it stood solely for the benefit of the appointed Station Master.

The main station building then presented a smart appearance, and aside from the usual offices and staff facilities, afforded accommodation for 1st, 2nd, and 3rd class passengers - the modern phrase 'customers' seems hardly appropriate, and no doubt of particular importance was also a store for foot warmers. All of this was on the 'up' or Newbury side of the line, the opposite platform hardly more than a flat ramped area and devoid of buildings save the signal box, as for the present all trains would arrive and depart from the one side.

Aesthetically also the station was well contained, a tunnel at the north end under St. Giles Hill, (- where years earlier cheese-markets had been held, hence the connotation in later years of 'Cheesehill' and later still 'Chesil'), whilst to the south there was first a high level bridge carrying a footpath from nearby Chesil Street to St Giles Hill and beyond this a road over-bridge at the intersection of Chesil Street, Bar End Road, Quarry Road and Wharf Hill.

The chronic shortage of funds available to the directors of the DNS had meant the only land available to them for their railway was at the then extremity of Winchester, and with much of this in the control of the Cathedral and College. What private land was required to be purchased was often also only provided after sudden and dramatic price increases.

Accordingly the site for the railway was necessarily hewn from the side of St Giles Hill. A swath of chalk was removed from the west side of the hill at the foot of which nestled the station. Not surprisingly then it could at times be a dark and even foreboding place, a situation not assisted over the years when trains bound for Winchester were halted at the home signal within the tunnel, "......Sinister were the tales of country girls, stuck in the tunnel while waiting for Cheeshill's home signal to fall, with sulphurous fumes swirling in through the open windows made eerie by the gas lighting........" - more than a grain of truth perhaps and recounted from George Behrend in his classic work. *Gone With Regret.*

But all that would be in the future and following on from the festivities of the day and which included also a sumptuous luncheon in the Guildhall, the little DNS attempted to occupy itself in gaining some revenue from its new route as well as galvanising opinion into the merits of achieving its original goal.

Suffice to say it was in the main unsuccessful, a recently discovered document from around July 1884 proving that the GWR were at one time possibly considering support for an extension of the route to Southampton, although with the tantalising header, 'Private and Confidential.' Was it then that the mighty GWR were doubtful of the worth of independent access to the coast? Unlikely, more like they were wary that for the present an uneasy truce existed with their main rival in the south, the L&SWR, and to openly provide support for a venture into the very heart of the rivals camp could very well lead to difficulties at perhaps more important points of interchange where the two companies were forced to co-exist. Offset against this was the lucrative traffic that could be gained from and to Southampton, the L&SWR monopoly of the Hampshire Coast not necessarily popular with its principal customers.

Certainly behind the scenes the DNS would have been keen to capitalise in any way with any group that would support it. The GWR in the meantime - and who by agreement continued to operated the little line throughout its independent life, well aware that sooner or later the DNS would have to cease its terminus existence, it was only a matter of time as to whether Southampton was reached with or without their assistance. The other, and equally valid consideration was a possibility of a sell-out to the L&SWR and which could then mean that company securing running rights into established GWR territory.

4 July 1884.

PRIVATE AND CONFIDENTIAL.)

5 PER CENT. DEBENTURE STOCK.

EXTENSION OF
THE GREAT WESTERN RAILWAY SYSTEM
to SOUTHAMPTON,
being a **NEW** and **DIRECT ROUTE** to and from **LONDON** (Paddington)

AND

to and from **SOUTHAMPTON** and **BIRMINGHAM, MANCHESTER,** and **SCOTLAND.**

Issue of £200,000
5 PER CENT. DEBENTURE STOCK OF
THE DIDCOT NEWBURY AND SOUTHAMPTON RAILWAY COMP^Y.

INCORPORATED BY SPECIAL ACTS OF PARLIAMENT.

DIRECTORS.

Chairman, JAMES STAATS FORBES, ESQ., Chairman London, Chatham, and Dover Railway Company.

Deputy-Chairman, JOHN WALTER, ESQ., M.P. (Berks), Bearwood, Wokingham, Berks.

LIEUT.-COL. SIR ROBERT JAMES LOYD LINDSAY, K.C.B., V.C., & M.P. (Berks), Lockinge House, near Wantage, Berks.

VISCOUNT BARING, M.P. (Winchester), Stratton Park, Winchester.

HENRY LEE, ESQ., M.P. (Southampton), Sedgley Park, Prestwich, Manchester.

GEORGE PALMER, ESQ., M.P. (Reading), The Acacias, Reading.

JOHN HENRY COOKSEY, ESQ., Kingsbridge House, Southampton.

GEORGE THOMAS HARPER, ESQ., Portswood, Southampton.

WILLIAM HOWLEY KINGSMILL, ESQ., Sydmonton Court, Newbury.

WILLIAM GEORGE MOUNT, ESQ., Wasing Place, Reading.

THE Directors of the DIDCOT, NEWBURY, AND SOUTHAMPTON RAILWAY COMPANY are prepared to receive applications for £200,000 Five per cent. Debenture Stock at Par, payable as follows :—

£10 per cent.		payable	on Application,
15	,,	,,	on Allotment,
25	,,	,,	on 1st October, 1884.
25	,,	,,	on 1st January, 1885.
25	,,	,,	on 1st April, 1885.
£100			

Interest at Five per cent. per annum will accrue immediately on each instalment from the date of payment thereof, subscribers being at liberty to pay up their subscriptions in full on any date when an instalment becomes payable.

This issue will be specially applied to ensure the completion of the line to Winchester, and be applied wholly to that object, any surplus being available for the extension to Southampton.

It perhaps comes as no surprise then that behind the scenes the GWR and LSWR came to a private - and unwritten arrangement, whereby the LSWR funded a final 2-mile extension from Winchester to a junction forming a connection with the existing L&SWR near Shawford and on the single condition that the DNS renounce all aspirations for an independent route to Southampton. To the DNS there was really no option but to agree and accordingly a new line from Bar End to Shawford (Junction) was opened without ceremony on 1st October 1891.

The requisite inspection of the new works was carried out by Maj. Gen. Hutchinson for the Board of Trade on 5th September and at which point a number of minor modifications were noted as being required. Amongst these was a white painted background on the brickwork of East Hill Bridge to assist drivers in sighting the red arm of the Down Starting signal against the brickwork. This was duly painted, and although much fading has ensued, the remnants of this paint are still visible today. In the brief note that accompanied the re-inspection report of 27th September, was also included a tantalising reference, "A signal cabin has been substituted for the ground-frame referred to in the report and has formed the subject of a separate inspection." This is the only reference ever found to this signal box and its, existence, location, use and lifespan will now no doubt forever remain conjecture.

Outwardly one of the most visible signs of the new line was the spectacular 32 arch brick viaduct spanning the River Itchen and water meadows at Hockley south of Winchester and which remains today a lasting reminder to Victorian civil engineering prowess. (The viaduct was one of the first of its type in the country to be built of concrete supplemented by a brick skin. Despite the progression of countless trains of far heavier weights than its designers could ever have envisaged, it is still as straight and true today as when built. Likewise there is no record of it ever having required major maintenance, and whilst the past four decades have seen it basically abandoned it has in recent times perhaps found a new role as a screen against road traffic on the adjacent M3 Motorway.)

For reasons that are not completely clear, the extension of the route southwards did not automatically mean the second platform at Winchester was brought into use for passenger traffic immediately. Indeed despite a rudimentary wooden shelter and a footbridge being authorised on 27 August 1891- at an estimated cost of £742 10s, work was not commenced at once and in February / March 1892 discussion was still taking place as to the most suitable positions for these structures. For the first few months then all trains continued to use the single up platform. Despite the limited service of just four passenger trains and one goods train each way daily, this would still no doubt have caused some

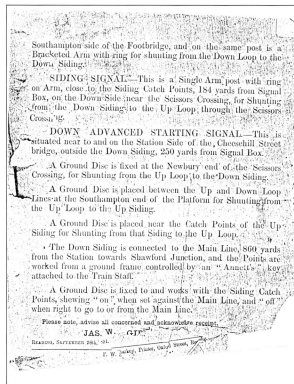

operational difficulties although hardly on the scale that took place only a few weeks later when a major earth slip occurred to the cutting side behind the down platform and which was graphically described in the Hampshire Chronicle;

"Saturday, November 21 1891. Winchester - A very serious occurrence happened at the Great Western Railway during the early hours of Thursday morning, which, had it taken place during the daytime, would more likely caused great loss of life. As is well known - perhaps too well known, for its existence has quite spoilt the view of St. Giles Hill from the City - there is a deep and almost perpendicular cutting on the east side of the railway, some 80' above the ground, the station standing on the west side, where a vast amount of chalk had to be cleared away to allow of the making of the building and its approach. The spot was visited at about half-past eleven at night when nothing had happened, but about 4 o'clock in the morning the occupants of a residence not far off heard a heavy crash, but as the wind had been blowing hard in the night no notice was taken of the occurrence. However, soon after 5 o'clock, Police Constable Stone was on his beat on St. Giles Hill and seeing what had occurred he at once proceeded to the residence of the Station Master and aroused him. Mr. Jeans quickly got up and went to the station, where he found a mass of chalk, since estimated at 1,550 loads with about 60' of the fencing of St. Giles Hill and a portion of the path had fallen to the ground, carrying with it about 100' in length of a brick wall of a good height and nearly three feet in thickness which had been erected to stay the progress of an ordinary fall of chalk from the bank. Three gas lamps were buried, the telegraph wires were cut, and the signal rods broken, and the mass not only covered the down platform on the east and filled up the railway, but a quantity of chalk was thrown onto the up platform. It is probable that damage would have been done to the station itself had it not been for the existence of the wall opposite. Mr. Jeans acted with commendable promptitude; he first blocked the line both ways and then got his staff together, and they with the assistance of about a dozen navvies who happened to at work in the neighbourhood set to work to clear the up platform and up line. This was accomplished by nine o'clock, and thus the through traffic was not further delayed. In the meanwhile Mr. Jeans had telegraphed Newbury, and as soon as possible a large gang of navvies was sent down and commenced work upon the mass of chalk and brickwork, an engine conveying the trolleys as soon as laden down the line. It is not improbable that ere long there will be a further fall from the bank a little more south, and it is hoped that every possible precaution will be taken in the

GREAT WESTERN RAILWAY.

Notice T. 473. (For use of Company's Servants only).

Chalk Slip at Winchester.

Commencing on Monday next, November 27th, Up and Down Trains will ~~work~~ in to the Up and Down Platforms at Winchester respectively.

This cancels my Notice No. T. 481; of November 27th, 1891.

Until further notice, Drivers of Down Trains must run to the South (*i.e.* Shawford) end of Down Platform before stopping.

Mr. KNUTTON, Winchester, to personally see that this is done.

Advise all concerned and acknowledge receipt.

JAS. W. GIBBS,

Superintendent of Reading Division.

READING, November 20th, 1893.

F. W. Starkey, Printer, 19, Oxford Street, Reading.

matter. No definite cause can be assigned for the unfortunate occurrence, excepting that the recent heavy and continued rains may well have had some effect upon the chalk. Barriers have been placed on St. Giles Hill and a watchman is on duty to warn the public of danger. The occurrence must incur an outlay of several hundreds of pounds. It is thought that the actual time of the fall of the 'avalanche' was twenty minutes past four o'clock, as it was found that the clock at the station, which had been duly attended to, had stopped at that hour, it is supposed through the vibration caused by the fall."

Piecing together evidence from the next years over the same matter and it becomes clear that the risk of further falls was being considered both in 1892 and 1893, for on 10 May 1893 there is a reference to a minute from October 1892 - which has not been found, and involving a tender received from Messrs. A Jackman & Sons for £900 in connection with sloping the back of the hill behind the station and restoring the footpath. An interesting aside is that Messrs. Jackman's had requested the railway grant travel passes to their men journeying from Newbury to Winchester to work on the cutting. This was refused, as it was "....against company policy." Extra expenditure of £125 on the work though for 'engine power' was approved, the amount to be debited to the DNS Company. The height

Winchester in the period prior to 1922 and seen from St. Giles Hill south. It is possible to identify the railway in the cutting at the base of the hill over 100' below and with the footbridge referred to from Chesil Street also visible.

of the cutting was also more accurately recorded at a maximum of 121'.

This however was still not the end of the matter for despite further remedial work in 1892/3 it would appear another fall occurred some time late in 1893 although the only reference to this is in the accompanying notice. This would appear also to have been the final slip of this kind although a century later the legacy of the falls may still be discerned even if partly hidden by the present Chesil Street multi-storey car park. A concave indent now shrouded in mature trees and foliage a permanent reminder of the events.

Possible concern by the railway as to the potential for injury to passengers due to another possible fall at some time may also be the reason a request from the Winchester Town Clerk for steps to the hill was rejected a few years earlier. This had first been requested on 20 November 1900 but was not finally refused by the GWR until March 1901.

Slightly back in time an interesting reference was found at the Public Record Office (PRO File 1057/82) dated 18 July 1892, involving a proposal for an additional siding at Winchester on the east side of the railway between East Hill and the passenger station. This it was suggested could be used for 'light goods traffic' and with a proposed holding capacity of 15 wagons. The matter was under discussion until October 1894 when it was finally rejected by H.M. Gipps, the DNS Traffic Manager, as he believed the proposal to be. "....too elaborate." Had it been acted upon an estimated cost of £990 was given, which included the necessary re-siting of the Up Home Signal.

Interesting to relate is that no alternative was put forward and aside from a very short extension to the private Simmonds & Gifford siding at Bar End in 1909, no additional siding facilities were ever provided at the Station or yard.

Another proposal some years later not acted upon was dated 11 October 1915 and involved a suggestion that the main station approach be altered so as to run to the rear of the Chesil Rectory and so emerge into Bridge Street opposite St. Johns Road. Why this change was even suggested is not mentioned although in any event no action was taken.

The 1892 proposal for the new siding facility at Winchester had no doubt come about due to the change of the DNS at Winchester from a terminus into a through route and in which there were other obvious benefits. Over the next few years traffic began a slow but recognisable build up aided by vigorous canvassing from the Traffic Manager based in Southampton as well as with the assistance of good relations formed with The Central Railway Company and whose tentacles stretched from Marylebone to Sheffield as well as a connection at Banbury. Accordingly from 1 July 1903 it was possible to travel by direct service from Southampton, via Winchester, Newbury, Didcot, Banbury and Leicester to Newcastle-upon-Tyne and where arrival was scheduled for 5.23 p.m.. For some years there was even a restaurant car attached for these through workings although in later years on this particular vehicle did not venture south of Oxford. The through workings would last, al'be'it in modified form

until 1939 - and it remains a tantalising thought as to the ability to take breakfast on the DNS line on a regular service train a century ago. (Slightly later in time, but a copy of the carriage workings for 11 September 1933 to 1 July 1934 reveals the formation of what was then the 7.33 a.m. Southampton Terminus to Newcastle-upon-Tyne service to have been made up of six vehicles. Monday, Wednesday and Friday these were, GW Van Third, GW Compo, GW Bk.Compo, GW Van Third, GW Dining Car, GW Van Third. On Tuesday, Thursday and Saturday the formation was principally LNER vehicles, as GW Van Third, GW Compo, LNE Bk. Compo, LNE Third, LNE Kitchen First, LNE Van Third. In both cases the last two vehicles in the list and which included the Dining / Kitchen car were added at Oxford. The Summer working was even more extensive and with no less than 8 vehicles in the GW formation and 9 in the mixed GW/LNE train. Six of these would work over the DNS.)

The earliest located view of Winchester following the opening of the line to Shawford Junction and with an LSWR Beyer-Peacock 4-4-0T No. 0321 at the head of four GWR coaches awaiting departure for Southampton. Compared with the view of the opening day on page 4, the additions of the footbridge and down side accommodation are noticeable, whilst it will be seen that the signal box has also been extended. This is likely to have occurred around 1891. It is not certain if at this time the single line instruments were in the signal box or as with the other stations on the line within the booking office and so under the direct control of the Station Master. The differing chalk faces of the hill after the falls will also be noticed. At this time all trains would change engines at Winchester although the LSWR did in fact have running powers as far north as Whitchurch. Whether they ever exercised these is not certain.

Adrian Vaughan Collec. Box 30/38.

Additionally from 1 July 1897 there had at last been the introduction of a through service between Southampton and Paddington. Leaving Southampton at 9.08 a.m. and Winchester at 9.40 a.m., it called at Sutton Scotney, Newbury and Reading, arriving at Paddington at 11.45 a.m. The return working was 5.45 from Paddington arriving at Winchester at 7.49 p.m and Southampton for 8.21 p.m. Initially advertised as a 'fast' but later scheduled to call at all stations - according to the DNS there was little point in missing out stops if there was the potential to gain the odd passenger. Even so the staff would still refer to it as 'the fast' for years to come. (It is dangerous to draw comparisons with today's 60-minute service between Winchester and Waterloo As a comparison the equivalent time in 1909 was in the order of 1hr. 45 minutes and so a time of just over 2 hours via the less direct DNS / GWR was still competitive. Unfortunately it was never as popular!)

One complication in the working at Winchester was the operational need to change engines of all trains at Winchester and due to this being the 'junction connection' between the DNS (GWR) and LSWR. Understandably also it was a time consuming and laborious affair. As far as passenger services were concerned engine changing took place in the platforms but goods could be dealt with at Bar End. From 1910 Great Western engines did commence to run through to Southampton but only on certain trains and the majority of services still continued to be dealt with in the old way.

Mr. Jeans, the Station Master at Winchester in post during the time of the chalk-fall, had also been replaced in 1893 by Mr. William Knutton. Mr. Knutton's tenure is also marked by contemporary records giving details of some of the more obscure responsibilities of a Station Master. Amongst these was to arrange for the distribution of gratis copies of the railway timetable, some, it was stated, in covers. A total of 67 were provided free to various outlets, including, Hotels, Refreshment Houses, certain public houses (including the 'Great Western' in nearby Bridge Street), Public Institutions, schools, the military and the Hampshire Chronicle. Delivery was by hand via the 'Outside Porter'.

Further publicity had been secured earlier through an agreement dated 20 October 1885, with George Lewis for Bill Posting at Winchester. For Bills standing for two weeks he was paid 2/- each and for those standing for three months he received 3/- each. He could also receive 1/6d per 100 handbills distributed.

The handbills and posters referred to would often be used to advertise forthcoming special workings and

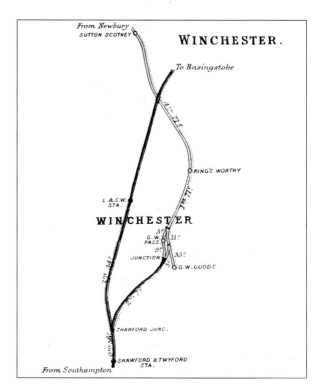

Taken from the official RCH junction diagrams, the junction between the DNS (GWR) and LSWR at Winchester is clear. The apparent double line in the area is explained as the station area and with what was in effect the down siding continuing to the supposed dead end at Bar End.

whilst they no doubt would have appeared almost from 1885 onwards, it seems the marketing of excursion traffic was far more vigorous from about the mid 1890's and no doubt connected with creation of the Traffic Manager post. Also from about 1900 onwards, details of special workings were to be found within the advertising of the Hampshire Chronicle. Destinations were varied and included London and South Wales although no doubt many would have involved utilising ordinary service trains and connections. As an aside one of the more unusual workings of this type was around 1910 and involved a trip from Winchester to coincide with a visit to the 'London Japanese Society Meeting'. Such special workings would continue up to 1939. The LSWR would also use the line for race specials to Newbury and which would then witness almost the only occasion when an LSWR locomotive would travel north on the DNS line to Newbury.

Stepping back a few years though and returning to the site itself, by the end of 1892 Winchester station was in a form that would have been readily recognised for the remainder of its life. Now trains would arrive from Newbury at the 'down' side and mostly depart north on the original 'up' side. A neat timber footbridge for passengers complete with canopy spanning the tracks. Also on the 'down' side was a small timber built and panelled waiting room but with only basic facilities. The reason for such limited accommodation on this side is simply explained in that there was little point in affording passengers much comfort if they were intending to venture onto another company's route - the L&SWR connecting line commencing immediately at the south end of the station.

Below; Winchester Station during the tenure of Mr. Knutton and depicted in the period 1893-1910, although probably towards the latter date. The neatness of the area is typical of the railway scene in this period in time and which clearly shows in the uncluttered appearance of the platform-even the barrow is neatly parked! One minor point is that at this time the chimneys were devoid of pots, these were added some time after 1919.

Kidderminster Railway Museum.

Within the main station buildings, the general abolition of second class travel in 1909 had resulted in the now redundant waiting room was from that class being re-designated for the use of first class passengers. The former first class waiting room was now to be used as an office for the Station Master who had previously either shared the station Booking Office or used his own private office in the station house and which overlooked the station approach. (As late as 1948 authorisation was given to redecorate the Station Master's office and which was referred to even then as 'formally the first class waiting room.') What was later the fish store at the north end of the platform had also once been used for heating foot-warmers for first class passengers.

Opposite the main station building was also the original timber signal box. This had been provided by Messrs. Saxby & Farmer and who as signalling engineers were also responsible for the necessary additional connections consequent upon the installation of the scissors crossover necessary with the extension of the line south in 1891. At this time the signal box was only just six years old and there appears some correspondence as to possible re-siting it at a new although unspecified site. In the event this was not carried out although it is believed it may well have been extended lengthways around the same time. In this form it would remain in use until 1922. At first manned by staff working a 12-hour shift, this is reported as having been reduced to 10 hours from 24 October 1910. At the same time the wages of the signalmen were increased from 20/- to 22/- weekly. The same year saw a reference to the introduction of Electric Tablet working between Winchester and Shawford Junction at a cost of £160. [The original means of working was 'Staff and Ticket'. A yellow coloured staff provided and with the wording ' Shawford Junction and Winchester (Didcot).'].

Behind the scenes the DNS, despite being officially barred from promoting the extension of their route south were however active in canvassing support from various disenchanted users of the LSWR in Southampton. The result was the formation in 1901 of a nominally independent concern 'The Southampton and Winchester Great Western Junction Railway', and whose proposed route would broadly follow the original intentions from Bar End through, Twyford, Allbrook, Chandlers Ford, Chilworth, Shirley and terminating at the Royal Pier. Despite early promise this concern was no more successful at raising interest and capital than its predecessors and by 1905 and when Parliamentary time had expired nothing further had been carried out. Had there been a mind this would have been the ideal time for the GWR to support the venture, they could also certainly have done so in a private capacity. Perhaps though their own expansionist

plans elsewhere meant there was simply not the will and accordingly this last opportunity was passed by. 1905 also marked the end of any extension plans for the DNS, it was to be the 1940's, and out of scope of the present narrative before any further major expansion was commissioned. (Had the DNS had the ability its expansion plans over the years were many and varied and included routes to Portsmouth, Bournemouth, Aldermaston, Quainton Road - near Aylesbury, Basingstoke, Chilbolton, Aldermaston, Vernham Deane, and Lambourn. The lack of success in raising the necessary capital should be read against a background where other railway schemes were over-subscribed - the Great Central London Extension the classic example. It appears then that the investment market was wary of railway schemes in more rural areas. The GCR may even have been considered as a potential partner to the DNS in certain of these as especially to Quainton Road, although that would no doubt have resulted in the GWR withdrawing from the established working agreement.)

Clearly the running of the various special workings over the years and referred to earlier was an attempt to augment the limited passenger revenue and which was otherwise derived primarily from local traffic. Indeed as can be seen from the accompanying figures it was for many years the goods services that afforded the majority of the revenue. These are taken from the DNS Minute Books and so present a detailed comparison. They do though relate to the whole line from Didcot to Winchester. Even so, for comparison purposes they are given here including the years from 1882 when only the section north of Newbury was open;

Another example of attempted additional passenger revenue occured on 6 January 1906 with the issue of cheap tickets from Winchester to Southampton for the football match with Norwich City. These were advertised at 1/3d 3rd. class return and were valid on specified trains only. A rider added that 'No luggage is allowed'. Of course the DNS would only gain a very limited return from such a working as for the majority of the distance it was off its own metals. Not surprisingly the LSWR would also advertise its own workings from its own Winchester Station and usually at a slightly cheaper fare! (There was no pooling arrangement for traffic between the LSWR and DNS/GWR for the route between Winchester and Southampton.) Even so similar football excursions were run for several years, the DNS unwilling to concede any opportunity for additional revenue no matter how seemingly paltry. It would appear football excursions were a common example of additional workings. A further example is recorded in January 1914, this time from Winchester to Wolverhampton and where the Southampton team were

Year Ending	Gross Traffic Receipts £.s.d.	Passenger Numbers	Goods & Minerals Tons / cwts.	Earnings per week £.s.d.
Dec 1882	5,807.17.1.	43,473	37,058.10.0	8.18.7
Dec 1883	8,632.15.1.	54,850	75,601.12.0	9.15.3
Dec 1884	9,187.4.5.	61,509	69,769.17.0	10.7.10
Dec 1885	13,087.8.11	99,824	81,367.7.0	9.0.8.
Dec 1886	16,101.13.10	130,130	86,909.19.0	7.4.0.
Dec 1887	16,542.19.5	131,134	89,178.4.0	7.8.0
Dec 1888	16,751.17.2	131,355	91,228.2.0	7.9.10
Dec 1889	18,302.19.2	141,443	101,435.4.0	8.3.8
Dec 1890	19,160.4.4	152,435	101,230.9.0	8.11.4
Dec 1891	19,515.16.1	137,384	113,229.3.0	8.14.6
Dec 1892	21,467.0.4.	143,515	136,951.16.0	9.11.2
Dec 1893	20,760.15.10	144,419	124,515.7.0	9.1.6
Dec 1894	22,379.16.6	162,418	141,154.7.0	9.15.8
Dec 1895	22,975.2.3	156,903	148,391.12.0	10.0.10
Dec 1896	24,217.2.7.	164,936	153,394.16.0	10.11.8
Dec 1897	26,243.9.1.	184,644	156,741.0.0	11.9.5
Dec 1898	28,033.6.0	188,263	161,256.10.0	12.5.0
Dec 1899	29,158.13.6	191,541	174,654.6.0.	12.14.10
Dec 1900	30,886.4.7.	199,763	173,980.9.0	13.10.0
Dec 1901	31,842.0.0	203,744	175,958.14.0.	13.18.4
Dec 1902	34,327.2.2	220,523	192,142.9.0	15.0.0
Dec 1903	34,613.18.9	225,566	211,280.8.0	15.2.6
Dec 1904	37,528.18.10	224,177	226,411.17.0	16.8.1
Dec 1905	36,422.9.10	223,067	214,264.8.0	15.18.0
Dec 1906	36,478.13.10	222,254	219,718.2.0	15.18.10
Dec 1907	37,617.14.4	220,922	233,674.10.0	16.8.10
Dec 1908	39,424.16.10	231,489	239,289.8.0	17.4.7
Dec 1909	40,825.5.9	255,550	248,491.13.0	17.16.10
Dec 1910	42,222.0.1	257,481	256,764.10.0	18.9.1
Dec 1911	42,110.6.1	246,401	263,795.8.0	18.8.1
Dec 1912	42,690.8.3	236,401	252,094.4.0	18.13.2
Dec 1913	44692.15.11	251,192	256,568.19.0	19.10.8
Dec 1914	44,465.14.0	Not	Available	19.8.8.
Dec 1915	44,741.19.10	Not	Available	19.11.1
Dec 1916	44,694.17.2	Not	Available	19.10.8
Dec 1917	44,750.4.0	Not	Available	19.11.2
Dec 1918	44,731.10.4	Not	Available	19.11.0
Dec 1919	44,737.14.9	Not	Available	19.11.0
Dec 1920	44,761.19.9	Not	Available	19.11.3
Dec 1921	44,882.15.8	Not	Available	19.12.4
Dec 1922	44,866.16.6	Not	Available	19.12.2

again playing. The fare was 6/6d, and with the train advertised as running non-stop from Winchester.

Yet further revenue of this type came from special workings in connection with the Winchester Pageant of 1908. This is first referred to in general correspondence from the GWR on 28 May 1908 and which included references to an additional excursion as well as further football special working later in the year. In so far as the Winchester Pageant was concerned, this involved a special working each day from 25 June to 1 July 1908 and which ran direct from Paddington at 11.01 a.m. calling at Whitchurch before arriving at Winchester at 1.02 p.m. The return was scheduled to depart Winchester at 6.45 p.m. non-stop to Paddington for an 8.36 p.m. arrival. It is believed similar trains may have been run a few years earlier in 1901 in connection with the millennium of Alfred the Great and also a celebration at Winchester College.

Around 1910 there was also much additional traffic handled in consequence of an Agricultural Show of that year, whilst records show that on June 11 1910, 200 baskets of strawberry traffic were loaded for Edinburgh. This consignment left Winchester at 3.00 p.m. and running via the Midland Railway reportedly arrived at its destination at 4.00 a.m. next day. Whilst events such as the Agricultural Show were really little more than 'one-offs' seasonal peaks were a feature of the workings for many years.

Whilst by 1914 the expansionist plans for the DNS in so far as Southampton was concerned were over, not so elsewhere, for on 13 May 1913 a document was produced - presumably by the DNS Traffic Manager, which details an ambitious proposal for a connection with the LSWR north of Winchester Junction - the point of divergence of the Alton Line from the main LSWR, and also where the DNS route passed under the LSWR, and which would have seen a loop provided to allow LSWR traffic to turn west to a connection onto the DNS south and so run via Winchester (DNS) before re-joining the LSWR at Shawford Junction. Obviously there is some bias towards the advantages to the DNS, but otherwise the information contained is accurate and gives some interesting, and truthful assertions as to the contemporary situation, including, "...The Didcot, Newbury & Southampton Railway is at this point (Winchester Junction) on a rising gradient, and, within a short distance of the bridge is practically on the same level as the LSWR. The time is approaching, if it has not already come, when it will be necessary for the LSWR to continue their doubling (- quadrupling would be more accurate) of their Main line from Basingstoke to Southampton. Certainly the time has come when the

line should be doubled (quadrupled) between Winchester and Southampton to meet the requirements of Traffic. The doubling (quadrupling) of the Line through Winchester would appear to be a very costly matter for the London and South Western Company, and this no doubt has deterred them from taking the work in hand. Their accommodation for Goods Traffic at Winchester is now very cramped and limited and the alterations to the Passenger Station and running lines necessary on any schemes of 'doubling' would materially decrease the accommodation. There does not appear to be any means of increasing the size or accommodation of the Goods Yard except at enormous cost. Moreover immediately south of Winchester Station the Railway runs through a deep cutting, with the Barracks on one side and the cemetery on the other side. It would appear therefore that any widening of the Railway through Winchester could only be undertaken at a very considerable cost. The provision of an alternative or relief Line for the London and South Western Railway could, it appears to me, be provided at a comparatively small cost by means of a Junction between the LSWR and the Didcot, Newbury & Southampton Railway near the Winchester Junction previously referred to. This Junction could be affected by the construction of a short line, from the LSWR, at or about a point three quarters of a mile North of Winchester Junction, to a point on the Didcot, Newbury & Southampton Railway between Sutton Scotney and Kings Worthy Station...... . The cost of this short line or loop, could not be very great, but it would be small indeed compared with the outlay involved in doubling the line through Winchester with the necessary alterations to Passenger Station, Goods Yard etc. etc.. By means of this Junction, the LSWR would have two routes for Through Traffic at Winchester viz;

The station approach sometime in the early days of the railway. Once more the stark chalk of the cutting side is so apparent whilst a comparison with the view of construction on page 2, some idea of the amount of excavation required on the west side can be gained.

Another early view of the station, and with what is also a gateway leading to the down platform from one of the numerous paths on St. Giles Hill. It is not known how much use this path had over the years and certainly in latter times was very much overgrown. The advertising hoardings are a prominent feature, and whilst these disappeared over the years some of the timber battens and likewise holes in the brickwork remained. The height of the retaining wall was not original and can be compared with the view of the opening on page 4. The down line has inside keyed rail and at a spacing of 12 sleepers per rail length. Of particular interest are the two lamps near the end of the up platform and seemingly facing in opposite directions. There purpose is not confirmed although it may well have been this was associated with the stopping point and consequent engine changing procedure.

Their own line through Winchester Station and the upper part of the town. Over the DNS Rly. through Winchester Cheesehill Station.

Both routes would converge at Shawford Junction from which point forward to Eastleigh the London & South Western Company have, I believe, land available on either side of the Railway for widening purposes. There would also be the advantage, so far as Winchester Traffic is concerned of the accommodation already provided for dealing with Passenger Traffic at Cheesehill Station and Goods Traffic Bar End, without any additional Capital outlay on the part of the LSWR. The DNS Company's Goods Yard at Bar End is a large one, capable of accommodating a large amount of additional traffic without any additional Capital outlay. The distance from the proposed Junction, north of Kings Worthy Station, to Shawford Junction would be about 5 miles 12 chains. If the proposal for the Junction and interworking is entertained, it would be necessary for the Didcot Company to double their Railway

between Sutton Scotney and Winchester, a distance of 6 miles 67 chains. On this Section everything is provided for a double Line and the cost of the doubling should not therefore be great. Independently of the additional Traffic, which we shall get if the proposed Junction with the LSWR is carried out, the doubling of the Line between Sutton Scotney and Winchester is urgently required for our own requirements. It would considerably facilitate the working and avoid endless delays, which now occur to our Trains. I should like to see the Section between Winchester and Shawford Junction doubled, a distance of 2 miles 16 chains, but on this section there is the question of the Viaduct, near Shawford Junction, which was most unfortunately constructed for a Single Line only. The cost of widening this Viaduct would I fear be very heavy". The document continued in relation to suggested likely financial arrangements as to working between the DNS, GWR and LSWR, and concluded with the rather optimistic statement, "The pooling of Southampton and Winchester Traffic."

There is no other correspondence in the records of either of the major players in support or rejection of this proposal although it may well have been that the events that followed 1914 meant an end to the suggestion. Conversely of course 1914 could have even seen an increased need for the idea after all! As it was a similar idea was put forward - and rejected again in the 1930's.

Interesting the writer of the document appears to have not helped his own argument in the statement that the doubling was needed for DNS trains as well and to avoid delays. If that were the case it is hardly likely much additional traffic could have been handled even if the connection had been made and the DNS doubled. (With the exception of the section from Winchester to Shawford Junction the DNS had been build to accommodate a second track from the outset even though only one was ever laid between stations.) Why also should there be specific delays only between Winchester and Sutton Scotney? More like if delays did occur then they would affect most of the line.

The years from August 1914 onwards naturally saw an increase in troop and other special traffic and culminating in the total suspension of normal passenger services between 6 and 22 August 1914 whilst a shuttle of military services ran continuously to Southampton Docks. Similar interruptions were to continue until the end of October 1914 whilst further special workings necessitated adjustment of the regular passenger service which would continue through the years of conflict.

With a return to peace, the DNS - still notionally independent, returned to its quiet existence without frill or fuss. It would be some time before there would be a demand for the level of service that had existed prior to 1914 whilst in many ways the pre-war standards would never be repeated.

Throughout its independent life, 1885-1922, the working arrangement that existed between the GWR and DNS meant that the little company was credited with a proportion of receipts, although the GWR were careful never to allow enough funds to be raised so as to threaten their own controlling operational interest. In this way the GWR were slowly able to require the DNS to modernise and upgrade both the GWR and DNS. Whilst there were little in the way of possibly visible outward signs, one example may be taken to be the rebuilding of Newbury Station in 1909-10 and which was completed mainly at the cost of the little DNS line and who in this way were required to fund a major improvement to what was destined to be on the route of the new GWR line to the west. On the DNS itself additional staff sections were introduced which were later superseded by token working. A slow procession of

replacement of the original rails was also carried out. All of this was debited to against revenue otherwise due to the DNS and so meaning the GWR were slowly but surely ensuring the route was brought up to their own standards. Publicly Paddington may, through its publicity department, appear to have been a 'Gentlemen's Railway', but behind the scenes it was also a shrewd business operative.

With the passing of the Railways Act 1921, the forthcoming Grouping of lines under the Act meant the DNS was effectively swallowed up by the GWR and who alone amongst the major railway companies of the United Kingdom would retain its individual identity. This meant the little DNS line was now owned by the concern that had been operating it for the past 38 years. Its ordinary shareholders were destined to receive nothing in compensation.

Visibly then there should have been little outwards sign of the new ownership, although the exception was at Winchester and where the GWR installed a new - some might even say revolutionary, signalling system. What today would be considered 'state of the art', and of course as it was planned before 1923 the DNS were paying the majority of the cost! On site, track work alterations were carried out together with the construction of a new signal box replacing the original timber cabin whilst a number of new ground signals were also provided. The 20th century had arrived at Winchester, if the engineers charged with the installation had but known it at the time, they were installing the forerunner of a signalling system that would later be adopted throughout almost all of the British Railway system.

Accidents and Incidents.

Despite the incidents of engine changing that occurred over the years and which routinely included two engines on the single line in the tunnel, no accidents are reported concerning this routine operation. (A conservative estimate is that this probably took place on something in excess of 55,000 occasions from 1891 to 1922). Indeed only relatively minor matters are reported over the years, the first on 6 March 1888 when an unreported and undefined incident involved a Mrs. A. Strictland. A few years later on 6 October 1897, it is known that a trespasser was knocked down by a train near Winchester, whilst on 10 October 1899 a passenger fell off the platform breaking a leg.

Incidents and accidents of this type were of necessity regularly reported to the GWR and a record kept under the heading 'General Managers Report'. Accordingly perusal of these records often gives brief mention of a happening but tantalisingly without further detail.

Accordingly, on 17 March 1921 a member of staff, Checker W. Stroud was hurt. Possibly Mr. Stroud was just unfortunate as he featured again, although once more without detail, on 23 October 1923. Another Checker, Mr. Hatter is similarly mentioned as having been injured on 11 May 1922.

The story of the staff at Winchester Station is both complicated and unique. Complicated by virtue of the number of individuals to be dealt with but unique because for the first time it has been possible to piece together a reasonably comprehensive record of the early years using a variety of sources. Principal amongst these have been the Great Western Magazine, local street directory's, official staff records and also personal memories.

Even so it would foolish to believe such records as it has been possible to compile over a century later are exact, and so the examples given should be read as a 'snapshot in time'. Likewise the number of staff located through research does not always conform with the totals given by GWR statistics, although here the explanation may simply be that numbers could vary within the actual year and the GWR statistics relate to what was probably the permanent establishment without reference to supernumerary individuals taken on to cover particular needs.

Aside from their normal duties as designated by title, certain men amongst the staff were also tasked with specific duties. One example being the Parcels Office Checker who was responsible for the various signal lamps twice weekly.

It would likewise be both time consuming and repetitive to recount information on every person known of by name and so for reasons of space full details are only given of the men in charge - the Station Masters.

The first man then recorded in the post of Station Master was Benjamin George Jeans. At this point it should be mentioned that the local Warren's directories for 1885 make no mention of the DNS / GWR for that year and consequently the first entries relative to the new railway appear in the 1886 edition. As the line opened in May 1885 it must be that the entries were retrospective and with similar criteria within the Great Western Magazine.

Under Mr. Jean's tenure the station passed from being a terminus to that of a through venue. It is known of course from the contemporary newspaper reference to the 1891 chalk fall that he occupied the station house, but aside from this is regretted that little else is known of the man. No doubt in his position as Station Master, Mr. Jeans would have been present during the opening celebrations, and which compared favourably with the conspicuous absence of the Chairman of the DNS on that day, J. Staats Forbes, his excuse being, "…pressure from other business."

Possibly the only area of conjecture appertaining to his period in office, and which lasted until the summer of 1893, comes in 1890 when an analysis of staff names reveals that out of nine staff no less than six were replaced during that year. Is this then co-incidence, or did some incident occur to precipitate this amount of change? It is accepted of course, that staff will invariably move as time passes, although no mention is found to confirm or deny such supposition in records from any source so far located.

The successor to Mr. Jeans, and perhaps the best known of the Winchester Station Masters was Mr. Knutton. William Frederick Knutton arrived at Winchester in the summer of 1893 and would remain at the station through the end of the Victorian era until finally departing in 1910. It was he who would oversee a gradual increase in staff from the 10 that were present in 1894 to 17 by the time of his departure. Some of these new posts were also individually reported in contemporary records, an example being within the Minutes of the GWR Traffic Committee for 8 January 1896 when it was stated that an additional porter would be provided at both Winchester and Sutton Scotney. A little later in August 1897 there is further reference that consequent upon the introduction of unspecified, "….new trains…", a (head?) guard was provided - this was probably the Winchester to Paddington 'express' introduced around this time. A final reference relates to another new porter post created in April 1898.

The career of Mr. Knutton himself is also of interest. Born in 1865 near Banbury he had joined the GWR in the Traffic Department there before moving to Devizes and thence promotion to the Divisional Superintendents Office at Reading. After this, in 1885, came a move to Oxford followed by a further promotion to Station Master at Culham in 1890 when aged just 25.

His move to Winchester followed, and some mark of his popularity can be occasioned by a presentation made to him by the Winchester Staff on the occasion of

Mr. Knutton at his desk at Winchester. Amongst the duties commensurate with the Station Master position was a requirement to submit a daily report to the Reading Superintendent as to any delays to trains and likewise their cause. There were several even with the limited service operating at this time, although most amounted to little more than a minute or two and were often ascribed to 'engine changing' or a delay in the arrival of the service from the LSWR. One of the more obscure though, referred to the 7.55 a.m. departure north one August morning and where it was recorded the train was delayed for two minutes due to, "...40 dogs for London which arrived late."

Kidderminster Railway Museum.

his marriage on 23 September 1897. To commemorate the event the staff presented him with an inscribed four-piece silver tea service whilst the wedding itself was reported within the Hampshire Chronicle.

"The Parish Church of Wyke was the scene of a very pretty wedding on Tuesday last, in the presence of numerous congregation, the bride being Miss. Jessie H. Good, second daughter of the late Mr. George Thos. Good of Winchester, and the bridegroom Mr. Wm. F. Knutton, the esteemed Station Master, Great Western Railway, Winchester, and the eldest son of Mr. Fredk. Charles Knutton of Grimsbury, Banbury. The bride, who looked charming, was attired in a white alpaca trimmed with white lace and ribbon, with tulle veil and a wreath of orange blossom; she also wore a double heart brooch and carried a shower bouquet, the gifts of the bridegroom. The bridesmaids (Miss J. Good, sister of the bride, and Miss G.E. Marsh) looked very pretty and attractive in their attire; they each carried a bouquet, and wore a gold St. Cross brooch, the gifts of the bridegroom. The bride was given away by a friend, and the best man was Mr. Frank Knutton, brother of the

bridegroom. The ceremony was performed by Rev. E. Firmstone, Rector, Miss Florrie Wright presided at the organ, and played Mendelssohn's "Wedding March" after the ceremony. As the bridal party left the church they were greeted with showers of rice etc.. The presents were numerous, costly and useful. The happy pair left by the 5.5 p.m. train amidst showers of rice and confetti and good wishes for their future happiness from friends and relatives, for Weston-Super-Mare en route for Torquay for their honeymoon."

Mr. and Mrs. Knutton would have made their first home in the station house, residing there until his promotion to Station Master at Evesham and which was reported in the Great Western Magazine for September 1910. A presentation to mark his departure was held in Winchester Guildhall on 23 October 1910 and at which he was presented with an illuminated address from the staff and 'a purse of £40' (This was a not inconsiderable amount for the period and for a comparison, and as was recounted earlier, the Winchester signalman had at the same time been awarded a wage increase to £1. 2s weekly.) Perhaps surprisingly there is no mention of the departure of Mr. Knutton within the Hampshire Chronicle.

Mr. Knutton's stay at Evesham was evidently brief and it is known his next move - although when is not reported, was to the post of Station Master at Salisbury. Again this was only for a short time for he was transferred in November 1916 to hold the position of Depot Master at Rotherwas Junction near Hereford. The same reference recounting that he was the holder of the 'Signalling Certificate' whilst it is also known he had a keen interest and following in both hospital work and the GWR Ambulance Movement. His duties at Rotherwas were to be in charge of railway work at what was also deemed 'Munitions Depot No. 14', or sometimes 'No. 14 Filling Factory'.

From Rotherwas he was moved to the important post of Station Master at Oxford in December 1918, each transfer being to that of a more important and responsible position. By now he was 53 years of age although his career was destined to progress still further when in February 1924 he replaced Mr. J. Lea at Reading. Mr. Lea had left on promotion to Divisional Superintendent at Swansea and indeed Mr. Knutton could have expected such a further progression in due course or perhaps even to that of Station Master at Paddington.

Unfortunately fate would deal a cruel blow for in April 1924 just two months after taking up his new role he underwent surgery at Oxford. Recovery and convalescence kept him away from Reading until July but he was soon taken ill again and died at his home in Oxford on 4 August 1924.

The funeral took place on 7 August at Christ Church in Banbury. The GWR represented by several of his former colleagues and there were floral tributes from the staff as well as the Southern Railway's Reading Station Master and Messr's C & G Ayres, a Reading coal merchant.

Almost as a postscript, a final entry appeared in the Great Western Magazine in January 1925 and which reported, 'At the time of the last illness of Mr. W.F. Knutton, formerly Station Master at Oxford, arrangements had been completed to present him with a testimonial to commemorate his promotion to the position of Station Master at Reading. The testimonial consisted of a wallet of treasury notes and an

A surviving record gives details of the Winchester Passenger Guards during the period 1910-13. At this time there were three men in post, Messrs. Gilbert, Aishfield and Wise. Other duties were covered by Newbury or Didcot Guards and also one of the Winchester Porters. William Gilbert had joined the GWR at Wantage Road in 1869 where he was reported as 'In charge of the signals and points." Promoted to Passenger Guard in 1875, he subsequently moved to Paddington and also served at Swindon a d Aylesbury and then Winchester from 1900 . For 17 years he took charge of the service to and from Paddington before retiring in the summer of 1921.

illuminated address containing the subscribers names. The Bishop of Oxford had undertaken to make the presentation but owing to the death of Mr. Knutton, this programme could not be carried out. Mrs. Knutton, who had been absent from Oxford for some time, recently returned, when the testimonial was handed to her privately.

Mr. W. Gilbert.

Number of Set (duty)	Time on duty	Time off duty	Train	From	To	Time due	Gross working hours	Remarks
AISHFIELD	12.05 pm	10.03 pm	12.16 pm	Winchester	Didcot	2.10 pm		Sole
No. 378			3.35 pm	Didcot	Oxford	3.59 pm		Sole
			5.58 pm	Oxford	Didcot	6.21 pm		Junior
			6.40 pm	Didcot	Oxford	7.03 pm		Sole
			7.44 pm	Oxford	Winchester	9.57 pm	10.00	Head
GILBERT	9.30 am	8.10 pm	9.39 am	Winchester	Paddington	12.00 noon		Sole to Reading thence Junior
No. 379			1.48 pm	Bishops Road	Uxbridge	2.33 pm		Sole
			3.30 pm	Uxbridge	Bishops Road	4.18 pm		Sole
			5.45 pm	Paddington	Winchester	7.59 pm	10.40	Sole
Porter Wise No. 380			7.20 am	Wednesday and Friday				
			8.02 am					
Porter No. 381			8.45 pm	Winchester	Newbury	9.46 pm		Sole Charge Mons. and Weds. only
			10.10 pm	Newbury	Winchester	11.13 pm		-ditto-

In a letter of thanks addressed to the subscribers, Mrs. Knutton laid stress upon the appreciation, felt by her late husband of their kindness to him, and mentioned that it was her intention to use the money to erect a memorial to his memory.'

No further information has come to light appertaining to any memorial. There also, matters might be considered to be concluded save for the fact that in 1998, Mrs. K. Williams, a distant descendant relative of Mr. Knutton, gave to the Kidderminster Railway Museum several unique items. These included several photographs as well as the illuminated address intended to have been presented when he left Oxford and which is itself a beautiful item, leather bound and folded and with the complete list of subscribers in neat copper-plate. Perhaps the most amazing survivor though was the four-piece silver tea set, the teapot of which was inscribed to Mr. Knutton by the Winchester Staff and presented at the time of his marriage in 1897.

Mr. Knutton was succeeded around December 1910 by Mr. F.C. Brooks and who had transferred from Challow. The 'F.C.' probably stood for Frederick Charles, although some reports also refer to Francis Culham. His tenure was destined to last almost as exactly the same length as his predecessor and whilst much is known of Mr. Knutton, little is known of Mr. Brooks.

The period overseen by Mr. Brooks of course was not easy. The end of the Edwardian era and a slide into war. Indeed this was manifest even on the GWR at Winchester and where men who joined the forces were replaced by women for the first time and in roles which had previously been considered to be a male domain. Miss. D.K. Rogers was the first of these around 1916 in the post of Clerk.

A particularly interesting feature of the staff numbers and posts around this time was the increase in the number of 'Goods Clerks'. Originally just one had been in post but by 1916 there were three and four in most years after that until 1921. The obvious reason was increased war traffic, although this cannot be confirmed as traffic statistics are not available for the period. It may also have been that corresponding increases took place within other goods grades and possibly due to the existence of the Winchester Camp line from 1918-20. A final thought in this area may well be as to how the actual line capacity of the route as a whole and particularly Winchester fared, especially if the presence of 3-4 clerks related to a corresponding increase in goods traffic.

Staff at Winchester circa. 1914 and under the charge of Station Master Brooks - seated centre. The view was reproduced in the July 1914 issue of the GREAT WESTERN MAGAZINE and was typical of numerous staff views from around the system which were reproduced in this way. No names were given. The young man seated at the feet of the lower row is Porter James Blake and who left the railway to join the war but never returned. It is apparent also that this was only a selection of the staff working at this period, Guard W. Gilbert for example is missing, whilst the street directories are also of little help in identifying men by this time and their previous practice of naming men and posts was already tailing off and by 1923 just the identity of the Station Master was given.

Opposite page; It just might have been....!

EXTENSION OF WINCHESTER BRANCH TO SOUTHAMTON

G.W.R.

FROM 3 MAY 1903 THE LINE FROM WINCHESTER WILL BE EXTENDED TO SOUTHAMPTON (ROYAL PIER)

THE FOLLOWING NEW STATIONS WILL BE OPENED ON THAT DATE;

TWYFORD, CHANDLERS FORD, CHILWORTH, SHIRLEY, SOUTHAMPTON (ROYAL PIER)

(THE EXISTING SERVICE FROM WINCHESTER TO SHAWFORD (LSWR) WILL ALSO CEASE ON THAT DATE)

FOR TRAIN TIMES SEE TIMETABLES.

James Inglis
General Manager
Paddington. May 1903.

When available again in 1923, the same statistics reveal Mr. Brooks was now presiding over an increased number of staff, no less than 18. Inflation had also taken its toll in so far as the annual wage bill was concerned, recorded as being £1,097 for 13 staff in 1913 and £2,997 for 18 in 1923. Mr. Brooks left Winchester in April 1924 when he transferred to West Drayton.

The replacement this time was Mr. E.W.H. Sexton - the forenames are not known, and who was reported as having arrived around April 1924 having transferred from Staines. Mr. Sexton would be in charge until July 1932 and it is perhaps ironic that less is known of the latter station masters at Winchester compared with the earliest in post.

What is known is that Mr. Sexton was known to have a fanaticism over cobwebs and perhaps understandably then was given the nickname 'spider'. For a while also the station staff were jokingly known as a somewhat ecclesiastical bunch and solely on the basis of some of their names. This arose as aside from Mr. Sexton, there was around the same time a porter, Mr. Dean, a driver Mr. Church, and the goods clerk, Mr. Evans - referred to as 'Good Heavens'

According to the staff magazine Mr. Sexton moved it is believed to Henley - although one report says the transfer was to Windsor, in July 1932 and was replaced in the same month by Mr. G.A. Slater who had come from Devonport. Mr. Slater's stay though was only just over three years as he died in-post on 7 September 1935, at the age of 56.

There now appears to have been a gap of a some three months, until the arrival of Mr. A.A. Arch from Thatcham in November 1935. The apparently 'Station Master less' gap may be explained by a slightly late report within the 'Great Western Magazine' or by the use of a relief man.

Again little is known of Mr. Arch. Although it would be fair to say that the incumbent from this period, aside from having responsibility for Winchester would also now be in charge of the other stations on the line as a result of the gradual removal of the station master post between Winchester and Newbury.

No apologies for repeating the use of this 1919 view of Winchester from elsewhere. This was the scene then almost in the final years of private ownership, although especially at Winchester where the buildings were nearly all also to standard GWR pattern, the traveller could be excused for not knowing it was in effect an independent company.
Credit; LGRP No. 8353

Chapter Two

THE POWER SIGNALLING

The choice for Winchester as the setting for the new type of Route Setting Signalling was interesting although easily explained. Most of the signalling at Winchester in 1922 was already over 30 years old and elsewhere on the DNS, the GWR had been replacing signalling equipment on a regular basis. Indeed in the years immediately preceding the Grouping, in 1921 the GWR had begun a slow process of renewal and replacement on the line - of course at the time still charged directly to the DNS. Paddington were certainly not slow to realise when eventual take-over did occur, and which was inevitably a foregone conclusion, far better to acquire a well maintained system.

With the Winchester signalling apparatus falling into the category then of, 'being in need of renewal,' the GWR selected the location for the first trial of the Siemens route setting system. Winchester was itself selected, not just due to the renewal aspect, but also because of its ease of proximity to the GWR signal works at Reading. At a time when train was the only option when travelling the system, it was important to choose a site which could be reached easily - and returned from of course, in a day. Additionally whilst no major difficulties were hoped for, had there been a problem, the restricted train service would mean that only a limited inconvenience would result. Finally, and whilst there is no detail as to the actual cost, a high proportion was also borne by the DNS themselves. The GWR could hardly loose.

Together with the Electrical Engineering firm of Siemens, a joint design was prepared between L.M.G. Ferreria of Siemens - and who had Patented the principals involved in 1918 - No. 125028, , and R.V. Insell of the GWR. The result was a unique route-setting system and where the operation of any of 15 levers would set up a complete route compared with the previous 'one lever - one individual action'

Regretfully the timescale involved in the planning and installation of the new work are not recorded, and the first formal identification of timescale comes with the issue of GWR notice No. E.1222 of March 1922 and which provided details of the new work to 'Company Servants'. This was standard procedure with all new signalling installations although on this occasion there was also some detail given appertaining to the system and its operation.

Whilst as stated above installation details and costing are not known, other information fortunately is to hand,

including the posting of two Linemen to Winchester to oversee the operation and who both had specific electrical experience. These were R. Pritchard and R. 'Bob' Warren.

On the ground the new installation involved the provision of a new brick signal box, externally to a standard GWR design and which was located on a new site south of the station and immediately opposite the loading dock. This was a small affair and had a floor area of just 17' x 10'. A cost of £482. 15s 8d is reported, although this excluded the new power frame. With the commissioning of the new signal box and signalling the old timber box was subsequently removed.

Additionally, track work alterations in the form of two pairs of turnouts replaced the former scissors crossover, again this was likely to have been planned regular maintenance and not connected with any difficulty arising from the installation of the power system. Five track circuits were also provided for 'proving' the route although these only extended within the immediate area of the respective turnouts and did not then cover all tracks. In theory a signalman could permit of a second train to enter the same section of line / platform under a clear signal if the first train was not fouling any of the track circuits. (The track circuits probably operated on the standard GWR low voltage system rather than from the main batteries described later. To use the available 24v supply would no doubt have resulted in wheel burns or even weld marks and there is no record of these having occurred.)

Inspection train at Winchester possibly in connection with the 1922 installation.

R.W. Kidner

Reproduced from the official GWR notice No. E.1222

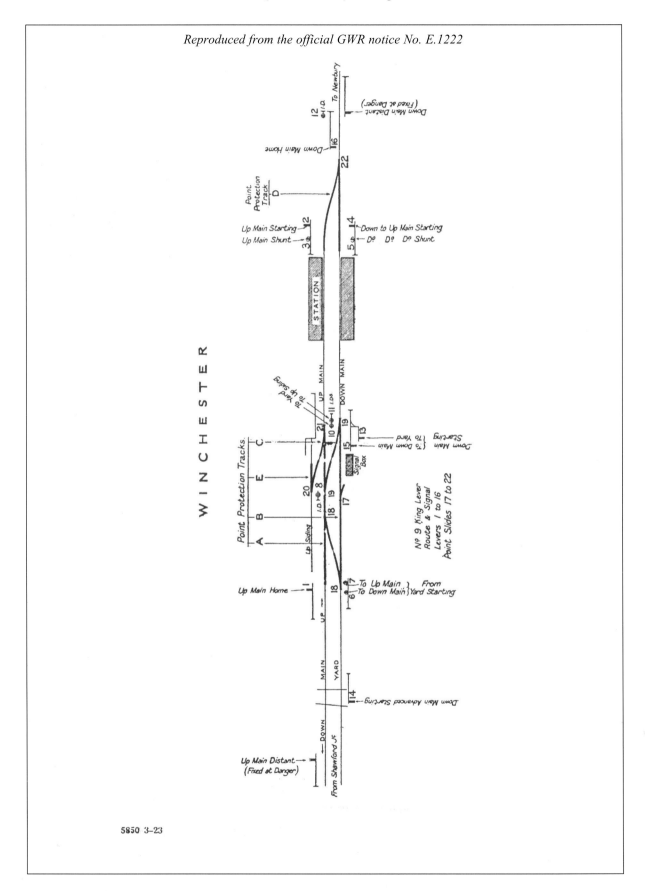

Being a relatively simple track layout, it was decided that just 15 routes would be required for all possible train movements and accordingly the frame was built around these needs. The operation of any one of these 'route levers' first checked the track circuits before moving all necessary points after which the appropriate signal would be cleared. Mechanical locking added to the necessary electric locks on what were miniature levers was still provided within the frame. Additional to the 15 route levers was a 'King' lever and which when moved, freed a number of individual point slides allowing for the separate movement of any of a number of the points. This though could only be accomplished when all other levers stood 'normal' in the frame.

The levers were numbered 1-16 as follows;

1.   Up main Home to Up main Starting
2.   Up main Starting.
3.   Up main shunt.
4.   Down to Up Main Starting.
5.   Down to Up Main Shunt.
6.   To Down Main from Yard Starting.
7.   To Up Main from Yard Starting.
8.   Up Siding to Up Main.
9.   King Lever.
10.   Up Main to Yard.
11.   Up Main to Up Siding.
12.   Single Line to Up Main.
13.   Down Main Starting to Yard.
14.   Down Main Advanced Starting.
15.   Down Main to Down Main Advanced Starting.
16.   Down Main Home.

Two further anticipated traffic movements were not covered solely by any of the routes set above and accordingly within the formal working instructions it was stated that a hand signal must be given to the driver under the following conditions;

"When a train from Shawford Junction is stopped on the Up Line outside the Home Signal for the purpose of picking up traffic from the Passenger Siding, after the vehicles have been attached and have been brought out,

The immediate change over period at Winchester in 1922/3 and with the new signal box and point work and the old signal box still visible on the platform. It would be removed soon afterwards. The photograph is also the only known view to give some idea as to the design of ground signal used. A point motor can also be seen in the 'six foot'.

Collection. J.D. Francis

Mr. Brooks again together with certain members of his staff and three others who are probably visiting engineers. The date is not recorded. Given the unique nature of the installation it would perhaps have been expected that a number of official photographs would have been taken by the GWR but these are conspicuous by their absence. The rumour has always been that the Signal Works at Reading did maintain its own photograph records but that they were destroyed years ago. Indeed the majority of photographs located are from other sources and so may then give some credence to this theory.

a hand signal must be given to the Enginemen for the engine and vehicles to set back 'Main line' on to the train.

When a train has been admitted into the Up Platform Line and it is necessary for it to be set back on the Up Line for the purpose of picking up or detaching traffic from or to the Passenger Siding, a hand signal must be given to the driver to set back when ready."

The points slides were further numbered in consecutive sequence;

17.   Catch Point.
18.   Up main to / from down siding (yard).
19.   Down main to single line.
20.   Up siding to Up main. *
21.   Up main to Up siding. *
22.   Up Main to single line.

* Nos. 20 and 21 each represented one end of a turnout

but were activated individually as slides as they were required to act independently as traps.

The four ground signals, Nos; 8,10,11 & 12 also acted as independent discs and were not activated directly by the movement of the respective point blades.

Point slide levers, Nos. 17, 18 and 20 had two light indications, green above and red below to indicate and which indicated those points which were automatically restored to their normal position by the reversal of the signal. Nos. 19, 21 and 22 could be left in either position after a train had passed and so were provided with green and orange indicators. In all cases the position of the points was indicated by a change from green to red or orange - or vice-versa. Additionally each point slide had a mid, or neutral position and which is where the slide would normally stand when conventional operation of the frame was in force.

Notice no. E.1222 also gave specific instructions as to

the operation of the frame for normal day-to-day working. "The signals and discs governing the various routes cannot be lowered unless the white 'track' disc behind the lever for the route required is illuminated to indicate that the point protection track or tracks concerned are clear. In pulling the signal and route levers, the movement from the first or normal to the second or 'route' notch sets any points governed by the signal in the correct position for the passage of a train, and the illumination of the orange disc is an indication that the route has been properly set. The movement of the lever right over from the second to the forth position will lower the signal, which will be indicated to the signalman by the illumination of the green disc and the extinguishing of the light in the red disc. While the train is passing over any points operated by the signal and route lever the light in the white disc will be extinguished, and after the passage of the train the replacement of the lever from notch four to notch three will place the signal or disc to 'danger', the green light will disappear, and the red disc again become illuminated. As soon as the white disc is again illuminated, which indicates that the train has passed clear of the point protection tracks, the lever may be restored to its normal position, which will, in the case of points which always stand normal, automatically re-

set the points to that position."

The ability of the signalman to restore a signal to danger rapidly was of course a fundamental precept although as stated it did not also automatically mean the points were similarly moved.

The same instructions laid out in basic terms the action to be taken in the event of a power failure. Power for the installation was from two sets of 60 batteries of the Chloride Acid type. These were located in the base of the box in the area of what would conventionally be the locking room. The batteries were kept charged by linking into the public supply once a week for about three hours, and which was controlled from a bank of switches within a cabinet on the rear wall of the box. The base of the box was also vented by means of a number of airbricks - there being of course no conventional point rodding or signal wires emerging anywhere. Fortunately the GWR were well aware of the risk from highly flammable hydrogen gas given off during charging. On the ground the system required either a 120v or 24v supply and either set of batteries could be switched to provide the requisite voltage. In practice changeover was made - again by switches in the upstairs cabinet,

LOCKING	TABLE	FOR	POWER	FRAME
Lever	Sets Normal	Sets Reverse	Restores Normal	Locks Normal
1	18,19,20,21			7,8,9,10,11,12,14,15
2		22		3,4,5,9,12,16
3		22		2,4,5,9,12,16
4	22			2,3,5,9,12,16
5	22			2,3,4,9,12,16
6	18,19	17	17	7,9,10,13,15,16
7	19,20,21	18	18	1,6,8,9,11,12,13,15
8		20,21	20	1
9				
10	19,20,21	18	18	1,6,7,8,9,11,13,14,15
11	21	20,22	20	1,7,8,9,10,16
12		22		1,2,4,5,7,8,9,16
13	18,19	17	17	6,7,9,10,15
14				1,9
15	17,18,19	19		1,6,7,9,10,13
16	22			2,3,4,5,6,9,12

The interior of the signal box and with the power frame installed. At the far end is the Tablet Instrument for the section to Shawford Junction, the release of a tablet being electrically interlocked with the down advanced starting signal. Nearest the camera is a the Token instrument for the section to Kings Worthy and with an Annett's Key at the end of each token for release of the Ground Frames at Winnall. At the far end, although more clearly visible in the lower view were lockers for use of the signalmen.

A close up of the 16 lever frame, all levers standing normal-the King lever also in its usual position. The frame was actually quite tiny, just 2' 10" x 2' 4" and standing a maximum of 4' off the ground. Published information refers also to just six operating slides and it may well be then that the seven seen were because the frame was of a standard Siemens type rather than being especially made for Winchester. A brass plate separated into 16 sections described the function of each lever as per individual lever leads. The same design of frame, although of necessity made up of several sections due to the number of levers required, was later used at the Newport installation.

every 24 hours and so providing for a uniform drain on the reserve. Maintenance was understandably the responsibility of the linemen and whilst in today's terms the whole system may be considered to be somewhat 'over-engineered', proof of its efficiency can be given in that throughout the life of the installation no cell failures were ever recorded. Preventative maintenance was the order of the day and with a shaped piece of wood carefully passed between the plates at regular intervals to remove any scale that had built up. The scale would then drop down to the bottom of each cell forming a small pile of sediment. In this way 'furring' of the plates was prevented. Over the years only two cells were noted as ever needing to be completely washed out. Protecting each lever circuit were individual fuses, again in the same glass fronted cabinet on the operating floor. These were colour coded for their different ratings. The signalman was expected to examine and if necessary replace the appropriate fuse should a lever fail to produce the requisite action. An

entry would then be made in the Train Register and the lineman advised.

Additionally a separate fuse cabinet was located at the entrance to the loading bay from Chesil Street opposite the signal box and which was where the mains supply was tapped from.

No. 9, the King Lever was unique, and strict instructions related to its use. For conventional working the King Lever remained upright in the frame and could be moved forwards to a position whereby the track circuits and back-locks were over-ridden. Similarly by pulling the King lever backwards it was possible to operate the individual point slides.

Whilst such a provision was undoubtedly necessary, it is surprising there is no reference to an inspection and comment by the Board of Trade on the system and the King lever in particular. Although the installation did

Part of the power control and supply equipment with the indicator dials to the top showing the rate of discharge of the batteries and also the state when charging was taking place. The signalman on duty was also expected to play his part and with the local instruction to, "...close main power switches Nos. 1 and 2 in the switchboard cupboards...", when coming on duty and then to open them before leaving duty. The switches were also to be closed if there was a long gap between trains as power could likewise be saved in this way. Before doing so however, all levers were to be placed in their 'normal' position. Due to the specialist nature of the equipment a particular skill was required of the lineman and accordingly it may well have been that this was also a factor in the later decision to abandon the installation at Winchester.

Taken from the RAILWAY GAZETTE article on the installation at Winchester and showing signals 6 and 7 and with their respective motors at the base of the post. The wiring in its neat wooden trunk is also visible although this was later said to be affected by damp and attacked by rats in places. To the left the two horseboxes are stabled in the up siding and would probably be due to be attached to an up train at some stage - hence the reason for the additional instructions in working referred on pages 28/29. Indeed the requirement to change engines of a number of passenger trains at the station necessitated the provision of more set routes than would otherwise have been necessary. According to the RAILWAY GAZETTE, in practice the signalman could set up a complete route in between 2.2 and 6 seconds, this being the time taken to pull the lever fully over from normal to reverse and for all the equipment on the ground to respond. Surprising then that the frame was not always popular with the men working it. Another advantage of the system was the way it would leave points in their last position unless they were required to be moved for the purposes of forming a 'trap'. In this way there was a material reduction in wear and tear.

actually record automatically on a special instrument - probably a graph, every time No. 9 was operated. The signalman would also be expected to record in the Train Register details of all failures and occasions requiring the use of No. 9, and if necessary also call upon the lineman to assist.

As already stated, a 120v supply was provided from the signal box and which was used to power the clutch driven motors for the points. Facing point locks operated in similar fashion and there were no fouling bars. Each set of points was also fitted with a run through spring to prevent damage to the mechanism should a vehicle pass in the wrong direction. Should an obstruction be lodged between the point blades then the design allowed the motor to slip to prevent undue damage.

The signal motors were slightly different in that they used either the 120v or 24v supply. The ground signals used the lower voltage and were in effect miniature semaphores of quite unique design. These were activated by a powerful solenoid the force of operation of which would have been quite sufficient to cause serious injury if standing nearby. (Contemporary records are at times confusing as in a Siemens publicity journal of the period a 100v supply for the signals is referred to.)

Altogether there were eight point machines, eleven signal motors and three solenoids. The latter number is despite the fact there were four ground signals, one being a double, and which was operated by means of a selective clutch from a single motor. (In recent years there has been some debate as to the accuracy of the contemporary reports in the use of a selective clutch driving a solenoid. It is possible then that shortly after being installed replacement motors, similar to those used for the signal motors may have been installed, al'be'it of a smaller type.)

Despite the availability of an electric supply to each signal, the signals themselves - with two exceptions, continued to be illuminated by conventional oil lamps. A yellow paraffin lamp placed behind the glass to produce a red or green light. (The green glass to the rear of the signal was in fact blue, and displayed green when the yellow light from the paraffin shone through it. This was standard GWR practice.)

The exception to this was in the tunnel where both the ground signal and down home signal were fitted with electric lights. It is not clear though where the supply for these came from.

In service the equipment was initially reported as being very reliable although the installation was stated not to

Part of the installation of 60 cells of the 'Chloride Acid' type and which provided power for the installation. These were located in the base of the signal box, hence the air bricks seen in the exterior photographs.

have been popular with the signalmen. The timetable requiring an average of perhaps 450-500 route settings per week and which was considerably less than the 2500 - 3000 that would have been needed for conventional mechanical working. Why the men appeared not to be in favour of the equipment is not reported as the majority of manual work previously associated with their role was now removed. Maybe it was simply a reluctance to accept change.

Only one failure over the years was reported, and when the 'stop' on the driving plate for a point motor broke off and so allowed the point motor to run continuously. In consequence the motor ran hot but otherwise remained undamaged. The Winchester Linemen arranged their own repairs with the aid of a local engineering firm who manufactured a new flywheel and it was installed and working within 48 hours. In the meanwhile a member of staff was deputised to manoeuvre the points, (- it is not known which set was affected) by means of an emergency winding handle, similar to the emergency provision of standard motor points in later years. Officialdom was also only told after the event!

Another change in so far as the signalling was concerned took place a very short time after the installation and although not directly related to the power system should be recounted for the sake of completeness. This was the interlocking of No.14 with the tablet instrument to Shawford Junction and which meant the signalman could not clear this signal unless a tablet had been obtained for a train to proceed in that direction. This had certainly taken place by early in 1923. In the opposite direction, towards Kings Worthy contemporary GWR practice applied, and the starting signals and electric token were not similarly interlocked.

Slightly further back from the scene on page 32, and this time with No. 1, the up home signal also visible. Aside from the electric motors, the signals were - apart from the ground signals, to standard GWR design. The ground signals, and of which there are unfortunately no close up views, the nearest seen being that in the illustration on page 27, unlike anything seen elsewhere on the GWR and so no doubt to Siemens pattern. The track work is interesting and consists of three bolt chairs on the running line (left), whilst inside keyed rail in 2 bolt fastenings is used on the down siding.

An unknown member of staff posed outside the signal box. At ground level doors were provided at both ends of the box , that to the right though was little used. The signal box name board 'Winchester Signal Box' would have been transferred from the original structure. Records show the plate had been ordered from Reading on 30 May 1894 and the same time as similar plates were sanctioned for the other signal boxes south of Newbury. Interestingly, that later fitted to the Ground Frame at Winchester had been ordered slightly earlier on 15 March 1892.

As would perhaps be expected there was much interest principally from the technical press following the commissioning of the system and with articles appearing in several journals including *THE RAILWAY GAZETTE, THE RAILWAY ENGINEER* and of course *THE GREAT WESTERN MAGAZINE*. After that however interest generally seemed to wane and with its reliability proven Reading (The Headquarters of the GWR Signalling and Telegraph department), took steps to reduce their costs. Accordingly one of the two linemen was transferred whilst the other now included responsibility for the electrical equipment of the signalling as far north as Enborne Junction. To this end a lad assisted him.

Away from Winchester one other installation using the Ferreira - Insell system was undertaken, on the GWR at Newport, Monmouthshire. The contract for this was dated 7 December 1923 although commissioning for what was a much larger site did not take start until 29 May 1927.

Nearer to home, Winchester remained operated by the system until mid 1933, official reports recording that the working of points and signals was changed from electrical to mechanical operation between 22 May and 9 June 1933. Services though continued to operate during this time and would have been dealt with by hand signalmen. From the latter date a conventional mechanical lever frame and locking replaced the Siemens installation and likewise the various points and signals were similarly returned to conventional mechanical - one lever / one movement.

Why the reversion took place is not 100% clear. It is not believed there were any major problems and whilst officially, "… damp from the cutting walls to the rear of the signal box causing troubles with the electrical equipment", was stated, the men on the ground refute that. Their recollection is that problems described this way are exaggerated, as difficulties here were occasional and then only slight. Possibly more of a damp problem existed in the fuse box at the entrance to the dock and where the mains supply was obtained from. What is remembered as an electrical problem was insulation breakdown from the quality of the cables provided and which were also on occasions attacked by the local rat population.

Nothing was salvaged from Winchester and although certain items may well have been taken to Newport for use as spares the majority was probably scrapped. The exception was a large drawing of the wiring and which reposed in the locking room under the frame in the box until at least 1960 before being unceremoniously dumped. Interestingly the GWR chose not to replicate the route setting installation anywhere else other than Newport and later re-signalling schemes retained the 'one lever one movement' principal even if electric power for points and 'searchlight' signals were used. In the end it was left to British Railways to adopt similar principals in the their first generation of power 'boxes and where a route was chosen by pressing an entry button at the point the train would enter the area of control and likewise an exit button at the end of its chosen route. The system then checked track circuits, moved points as necessary and cleared signals. Winchester then was an intermediate stage in design. Conventional mechanical operation would be modified further over the years and including a greater use of electricity for remote operations. Winchester was perhaps then the first clue of a revolution that would eventually see the demise of conventional signal boxes throughout the railway system.

Motor equipment for three sets of points, two facing and one trailing, all placed in close proximity. The covers have been removed for the photograph, and accordingly depict the detectors, the type of facing point lock installed and also the run through springs.

Railway Gazette.

Historically important and worthy then of a second inclusion from the original DNS work - page 28, the scene is probably shortly after the new installation and shows the new connections to and from the single line and down siding - leading to Bar End. To the right is the loading dock, accessed by road from nearby Chesil Street and where horse boxes and carriage trucks were dealt with. It was reported that buffer lock was a common feature when shunting into the dock and despite investigation by Paddington purportedly by sending down some brand new coaching stock for trial purposes, no definite reason was found. GWR records from 1910 referred to the length of the dock as 410' although this was totally inaccurate as the true size of the loading platform was 215'. The impracticability of the proposed siding of 1894 at this point - see again page 10, is again apparent.

Horse Traffic from Winchester and loaded at the dock, had, according to the Working Timetable only to be attached to the rear of passenger trains. Meetings at Newbury, and it was stated Lingfield, would see 'boxes attached to the first up service. This would usually be the 7.12 am up train and which was permitted to take 'tail' traffic - horse and cattle, from stations as far as Woodhay. This would then be forwarded on the 10.12 am from Didcot. A further note from early days stated that the 7.35 am Southampton and which conveyed through carriages for Newcastle was not to take 'tail' traffic.

Chapter Three

HARD AND DIFFICULT TIMES

By the early 1930's the railway at Winchester had assumed a role not untypical of a passing place on many quiet cross-country routes. The GWR, as both owner and operator of the DNS line, seemingly content to allow it to continue its quiet and uneventful existence as a potential feeder to its other services whilst providing also a useful community service at a time when competition from the road was hardly a serious consideration.

Accordingly there existed in 1932 a service of some six passenger trains each way daily, supplemented by an additional Saturday evening service and with just one train each way on Sunday. This latter service did not run beyond Winchester and so any passenger intending to travel on to Southampton would be forced to walk the mile or so from 'Chesil to the Southern Station.

In July of 1932 the Station Master, Mr. Sexton who had been in charge since mid 1924 transferred away was replaced by Mr. Slater from Devonport. At this time, 1932, there was still some 21 staff in the Traffic Department which included Clerks, Porters, Checkers and Goods Department Staff. Those not included in this total were from the Locomotive, Engineering and Signalling Departments. The annual pay bill for all 21 was just £2,576 and this was against annual revenue for the year from the station of £21,266. This could be further broken down into £1,983 for passenger tickets and equal to 16,926 tickets issued together with 14 seasons, £1,604 for parcels traffic and the remainder - of course representing the bulk of receipts, £17,679, for goods traffic.

Comparisons after 1932 are more difficult as GWR accounting began to include certain of the Kings Worthy, Worthy Down, Sutton Scotney and Whitchurch figures with those of Winchester. Even allowing for these however, the trend was for a marked decrease in passenger revenue fortunately allied to a corresponding increase in goods receipts. The figures then for 1937, record just 10,782 tickets issued at Winchester and with a total passenger revenue, including parcels of £1,908. Goods though equated to a further £27,810, although probably in the order of £8,000 of the goods revenue could be ascribed to the other stations. Again this was typical of the railway, where freight was the major earner and would continue to be so for some time still to come.

The 1930's then may well be regarded as a difficult time for the railway, and whilst receipts had been affected, they were at Winchester at least still reasonable. Elsewhere on the route the start of competition from numerous private carriers together with the first bus operators had led to certain of the stations seeing traffic drop off by an average of a third.

Despite this the level of train service was maintained at previous levels, the exception being the solitary Sunday train which ventured south of Newbury. This was the Didcot (depart 12.55 p.m.) - Newbury - Winchester (depart 3.20 p.m.) - Newbury (depart 4.40 p.m.) - Lambourn (depart 6.05 p.m.) Newbury (depart 7.45 p.m.) - Didcot service and had been run primarily for the collection of milk with additional passenger accommodation. It was withdrawn south of Newbury from 1932 and with the result that from this time on the only Sunday workings would be the occasional special or those run for by the Engineering Department.

Returning again to the freight handled, a fortunate survivor is a record of the goods workings between Bar End and Winnal Siding in the period 13 July 1935 to 8 September 1936 and which would have passed through the passenger station. This record reveals that trip working to and from the Gas Company at Winnal took place an average of three times weekly and with a total of around 31 wagons between the three trips. A considerable number of these would involve coal wagons owned by the colliery or coal merchant and including, Foster & Co, Birley Colliery, J.R. Wood, Hickleton Main, Forbes, Abbot, Firbeck, Brodsworth Main, York, Doncaster, S.W. Wilkins, Siddins, etc, as well as others whose names are not always easily defined. Additionally wagons owned by the various railway companies would be involved.

If passengers though were conspicuous by their absence, not so maintenance requirements, as witness a recently discovered file detailing necessary inspections and repairs to the tunnel. The first of these is dated, 16 August 1932 and records the dates of inspection to have been 14 and 29 July. (Previous reports have not been found including that for 9 March 1931 and which is referred to in the accompanying text. It is known that 'unspecified repairs' were authorised in 1923 and 1924 at £270 and £271 respectively, and likewise there may have been other inspections between then and 1931.)

For the GWR, Mr. F.T. Bowler - and no doubt from the Chief Civil Engineers department reported on Winchester Tunnel that, "Water is coming through the arch between 25m 8ch. and 25m 8 1/4ch. as reported in 1931. Scaling of the brickwork has taken place at

various places but is not of a serious nature. Hollow patches exist in a number of places and the worst of these should be pump grouted with cement….. (A total of 88' was reported.)….small patches of brickwork are also becoming loose. These should be cut out and renewed. Between 76chs, 50', and 5 chs. 50', the arch is bulged about 3" in lengths varying from 8' to 41', a total of 140', at a height of approximately two feet above springing on the up side of the line. Small patches of brickwork have been cut out, and it is found that all four rings of the arch are deformed, and a cavity exists between the outside ring and the chalk. The brickwork is loose. I am of the opinion that this bulged brickwork should be cut out and rebuilt at an early date to prevent further distortion…..Where possible the track should be slewed away from the repairs to allow the work to be carried out during ordinary time. Inspection carried out from a platform fitted to an ordinary truck." Shortly afterwards on 29 October 1932 approval for work at an estimated cost of £550 was given.

Later years revealed similar inspection reports, and which were also all carried out using the Gloucester Tunnel Van. In 1937 a further clue as to the original construction is given when it was reported, "….The springing of the arch at different points is bulging and sounds hollow, this is due to timber being built into the brickwork originally. This timber is now decaying. In recent years a good deal of timber has been removed and the springing renewed."
Accordingly between the years 1932 and 1939 the

tunnel was inspected on at least six occasions and incurred known expenditure of at least £1,370, its general condition being described in 1937 as only 'fair'. The last inspection, by Mr. E.C. Cookson and accompanied by Bridge Inspector A.C. Buckingham though, was by far the most revealing, "….While the sidewalls were found to be in fair condition, the roof of the tunnel was found to be very "drummy" and "hollow". A number of heavy shales of brickwork directly over the track must be removed. To determine the condition of the brick roof for repair or relining, I propose to cut some holes in the brickwork. After this has been done, I will report further with my recommendations………" "Trial holes cut in the crown at 24m. 78ch…….revealed that the arch consisting of four rings of brickwork - red bricks built in cement mortar, is in good condition. The hollow and "drummy" sound when tapped is caused by the omission of compo between the first and second courses of brickwork. The brickwork is in good condition and I therefore do not see any necessity to do anything to this "drummy" sounding brickwork. The heavy shales of brickwork directly over the track have been removed."

The previous few years concern then would appear to have been partly unfounded, and what is particularly interesting is a seeming ignorance on the part of the GWR as to the structural make up of a major asset on the railway. This though would not appear unique, as aside from plans showing levels, elevations and the

Opposite page; A historically fascinating view of the short lived Sunday milk train at Winchester recorded at 3.15 p.m. sometime in February 1933. The photograph was purchased for just £2 at a jumble sale and I doubt very much that its significance was obvious to the seller. What it shows, of course, is one of the former MSWJ 2-4-0's awaiting to depart to Newbury and beyond on the Sunday only service. This believed to be the only time a regular passenger service was scheduled to depart north from this platform after about 1892. The train had been instigated primarily for the conveyance of milk from January 1925, and used a Didcot based engine and crew. Initially the timings were Didcot depart 12.55 pm, arrive Newbury 1.38 pm. Leave Newbury at 1.50 pm. arriving Winchester 2.57 pm where the engine would run to Bar End and turn. Depart again Winchester at 3.30 pm arriving Newbury 4.37 pm. Running tender first then to Lambourn the departure time was 4.50 pm arriving Lambourn 5.33 pm. Departure this time was 6.15 pm arriving at Newbury 6.58 pm. There was then a lay-over until departure for Didcot at 7.45 p.m. arriving at 8.37 pm.. Minor variations were made to the timings over the years although throughout its existence the service called at all stations en-route. The GWR no doubt hoped to attract some passenger patronage, but in practice this was extremely limited south of Newbury. Surprisingly the service persisted in its entirety until about 1940 after which it continued for some years purely as a Didcot - Newbury - Lambourn and return working. Referring again to the photograph, and accompanying the print was a note from the Railway Photographic Society and to whom the original photographer, B.J. Piercey had submitted the print - was this a competition entry? His notes give the technical details of the shot and also add the comments that the day was '...dull as ditchwater and cold...', he continued that this was, '...the only train of the day....not a single person got out or in, nevertheless corridor stock of modern design.' Some of the comments from the RPS on their 'Criticism Sheet' were also attached and included, 'A negative worthy of being carefully preserved as I believe this station has been or will be closed.', others were somewhat critical of the composition and / or print quality, although decades later it is of course historically unique. Possibly the former comment referred to contemporary correspondence on abandoning the route south of Winchester Junction around this time. (The 1911 the timetable showed a Sunday, Reading - Winchester service but in the down direction only.)

Dean Goods No. 2346 awaiting to depart north from Winchester sometime in the 1930's

Taken from the same location, although this time it is No. 3255 'Excalibur' leading a Newbury train.

standard 2 chain survey, no plans detailing the structures, bridges or original buildings appear to have survived and so there is every likelihood such resources were similarly not available to the engineers sixty years ago. The GWR though were quick to learn, and although slightly beyond the period covered by this work, it is worth mentioning that in the subsequent decade from 1939 to 1949 - the last years for which papers are available, every report stated, "Upon examination the tunnel was found to be in good condition......". With one exception also, in 1946, when £163 was spent on three patches of defective brickwork, no expenditure was required.

After 1939 the changes that affected the DNS both as route and also at Winchester were considerable. Additional traffic, a normal service curtailed or suspended, and an extension of the loop and signal box. All these would come about due to the upheavals of the time and are out of the period covered by this brief narrative. The railway of the period 1885-1939 would be gone for ever, its stable local traffic ignored or curtailed, its demise after that an inevitable conclusion.

DIDCOT, NEWBURY, WINCHESTER AND SOUTHAMPTON.

Miles.		Week Days. a.m.	a.m.	a.m.	a.m.	p.m.	p.m.	p.m.	p.m.	Sun. a.m.
	London (Padd.) dep	.	5 30	8 40	11C15	1 45	3 35	5 15	Saturdays only.	11 0
...	Reading ...... ,,	...	6 52	9 28	11 40	2 35	4 58	6 8		12 10
.	Oxford . . ,,	.	7 12	9 50	11 20	2 50	5 0	6 5		10 25
...	Didcot ...... dep	...	7 38	10 20	12 35	3 35	5 53	6 47		12 55
3	Upton & Blewbury ,,	.	7 46	10 28	12 42	3 43	6 0	6 54		1 3
6¾	Churn ...... ,,	...	7 53	X	X	X	X	X		...
8½	Compton . ,,	.	7 58	10 40	12 56	3 55	6 14	7 7		1 16
10½	Hampstead Norris ,,	...	8 3	10 45	1 1	4 0	6 20	7 12		1 22
13½	Hermitage . ,,	.	8 13	10 53	1 8	4 10	6 27	7 23		1 30
18	Newbury ... arr	...	8 21	11 4	1 16	4 18	6 35	7 35		1 38
.	London (Padd.) dep	.	7 15	10 45	12 30	2 45	6 0	.	*7 55*	9 30
...	Reading ... ,,	...	8 28	11 50	1 17	3 32	6 8	...	*8 45*	10 20
.	Newbury . dep	7 45	9 5	12 25	2 0	4 28	7 13	.	*10 20*	1 50
21¼	Woodhay ... ,,	7 53	9 16	12 33	2 8	4 37	7 21	...	*10 28*	1 59
23½	Highclere . ,,	8 5	9 22	12 38	2 14	4 43	7 27	.	*10 34*	2 6
25½	Burghclere D ... ,,	8 10	9 27	12 43	2 19	4 48	7 32	. .	*10 39*	2 12
28	Litchfield (Hants) ,,	8 16	9 33	12 48	2 25	4 54	7 38	.	*10 45*	2 18
31¾	Whitchurch (Hants) W	8 23	9 40	12 55	2 33	5 1	7 45	...	*10 52*	2 25
37½	Sutton Scotney . ,,	8 36	9 50	1 4	2 47	5 11	7 55	.	*11 2*	2 36
40¼	Worthy D'wn P'form ,,	8 42	9 56	1 10	2 53	5 17	8 1	...	...	...
42½	King's Worthy . ,,	8 47	10 1	1 15	2 58	5 22	8 6	.	*11 12*	2 47
44¼	Winchester¶ arr	8 51	10 5	1 19	3 2	5 26	8 10	...	*11 16*	2 51
...	Winchester¶ dep	8 58	10 15	1 25	3 8	5 31	8 25	.	.	.
47½	Southern Rly. Shawford ... arr	9 5	10 22	1 32	3 15	5 38	8 32	...	...	...
51½	Eastleigh . ,,	9 13	10 29	1 39	3 22	5 45	8 39	.	.	.
53½	Swaythling ,,	9 20	10 37	2J 1	3A39	5 56	8 47	...	...	...
55	St. Denys ,,	9 24	10 41	2J 5	3 32	6 0	8 51	.	.	.
56	Northam ... ,,	9 28	10 45	2J10	3 36	6 4	8 55	...	...	...
56¾	Southampton Terminus§ ,,	9 32	10 49	2J14	3 40	6 8	8 59	.	.	.

	Week Days. a.m.	a.m.	a.m.	a.m.	a.m.	p.m.	p.m.	p.m.	p.m.	Sun. p.m.
Southern Rly. Southampton Terminus§ dep	.	.	P 7 33	9 40	11 30	1 47	4 52	7 30	Sats. only.	.
Northam ... ,,	...	...	7 36	9 43	11 33	1 50	4 55	7 33		...
St. Denys . ,,	.	.	7 40	9 47	11 37	1 54	4 59	7 37		.
Swaythling ,,	...	...	7 44	9 51	11 41	1 58	5 3	7 41		...
Eastleigh . ,,	.	.	7 51	9 58	11 48	2 9	5 10	7 48		.
Shawford ... ,,	...	...	8 0	10 6	11 56	2 18	5 18	7 56		...
Winchester¶ arr	.	.	8 8	10 14	12 4	2 26	5 26	8 4		.
Winchester¶ dep	...	7 5	8 16	10 23	12 10	2 28	5 33	STOP	*8 50*	3 20
King's Worthy . ,,	.	7 14	8 22	10 29	12 16	2 34	5 39	.	*8 56*	3 26
Worthy D'wn P'form ,,	...	7 19	8 27	10 34	12 21	2 39	5 44	...	R	...
Sutton Scotney ,,	.	7 27	8 35	10 42	12 28	2 46	5 51	.	*9 8*	3 37
Whitchurch (Hants) W	...	7 37	8 45	10 52	12 39	2 56	6 1	...	*9 18*	3 47
Litchfield (Hants) ,,	.	7 47	8 53	11 1	12 50	3 4	6 9	.	*9 26*	3 55
Burghclere D ... ,,	...	7 57	9 0	11 8	12 56	3 10	6 15	...	*9 32*	4 2
Highclere . ,,	.	8 4	9 7	11 13	1 1	3 15	6 20	.	*9 37*	4 8
Woodhay . . ,,	...	8 15	9 15	11 18	1 6	3 20	6 25	...	*9 42*	4 14
Newbury . arr	. .	8 22	9 22	11 28	1 15	3 27	6 32	.	*9 50*	4 21
Reading ..... arr	...	9 12	10C13	12 7	2 3	4 43	7 15	...	...	8 14
London (Padd) ,,	.	10 0	10 50	12 55	2 55	5 30	8 10	p.m.	.	9 17
Newbury ... dep	6 45	8 25	9 28	...	1 45	4 0	7 11	8 12	*10 20*	7 50
Hermitage . ,,	6 55	8 40	9 37	.	1 54	4 11	7 21	8 21	*10 29*	8 0
Hampstead Norris ,,	7 2	8 47	9 44	...	2 1	4 18	7 28	8 28	*10 36*	8 8
Compton . . ,,	7 7	8 52	9 50	.	2 7	4 24	7 33	8 34	*10 42*	8 16
Churn ...... ,,	...	K	K	...	K	K	K	K	...	...
Upton & Blewbury ,,	7 17	9 3	10 0	.	2 17	4 36	7 44	8 44	*10 52*	8 27
Didcot ...... arr	7 24	9 10	10 6	...	2 23	4 42	7 53	8 50	*10 58*	8 42
Oxford . . arr	8 32	10 12	10 37	.	3 18	5 25	8 30	9 16	*11 30*	9 39
Reading ..... ,,	8 17	9C39	11 5	...	3 28	5 25		9 37	*1‡42*	9 14
London (Padd.) ,,	9 0	10 15	11 55	.	5 22	6 15	.	10 55	*2‡40*	10 0

A—Change at Eastleigh. C—Slip Carriage. D—Station for Kingsclere (3¾ miles). J—Change at Eastleigh. Arr. 29 mins. later on Sats. K—Calls to pick up or set down Passengers on previous notice to the Station Master at Newbury. Evening trains call during daylight only. P—Through Train Southampton to York, Newcastle-on-Tyne, Edinburgh and Glasgow. R—Calls to set down on notice to the Guard at Winchester. W—About 1½ miles from Southern Rly. Station. X—Calls to pick up or set down Passengers on previous notice to the Station Master at Didcot. Evening trains call during daylight only. ‡—Sunday morning. §—For Docks. ¶—Cheesehill Station. About 1 mile from Southern Rly. Station.

The passenger timetable for the summer of 1932, and indicating six regular passenger trains on weekdays together with an additional service on Saturday and the erstwhile Sunday train. Not shown of course are any special workings although some photographic examples of these are recorded on the following two pages. Similarly the goods workings are not shown although there were usually two goods services in each direction daily. One of these would be the pick up goods, calling as necessary at each station on the line whilst additionally there was a 'fast' goods each way daily. That in the down direction arrived from Didcot - for many years commencing its run at 4.15 am, whilst in the reverse direction there was the 6.15 pm fast goods to Reading. This latter service would not call at the other wayside stations except to change tokens and so any goods from elsewhere on the line would have to be worked to Winchester first for adding to this train. A cruel comparison is to divide the number of tickets issued at Winchester in 1932 - 16,926, against the number of trains run. Taking a 52 week period and dividing this further into six days and 12 trains per day (six each way), and we arrive at a figure of just 4.5 passengers originating from Winchester per train. Naturally there would be others already on these trains and who had purchased their tickets elsewhere- a total of 57,458 for the DNS in total, but even if the original figure were multiplies by four to compensate it still represents a very poorly used service. Naturally there would be peaks as well and some of the trains would we well filled , particularly on shopping and market days, although to offset this other trains would perhaps have fewer passengers than could be counted on the fingers of one hand. Whilst not strictly within the period described by the present chapter, but certainly within the remit of this book, is a record of the working of Winchester in the 1920's period and compiled in connection with the building of the model of Winchester Station and which is now in a permanent home at Milestones Museum Basingstoke. It is reproduced on pages 45 and 46 .

26 March 1937, and a ramblers excursion at Winchester. The stock is interesting being some of the latest Great Western design and from its condition almost brand new. The number of vehicles is not reported although possibly in the order of eight. In the lower view, taken on the same day, the tail end of the train is now past the end of the up platform, whilst the signal box shows its recent change to conventional mechanical working as witness the point rodding.

T. Middlemas Collec.

Another excursion, this time a Sunday special from Winchester to Paignton sometime between 1932 and 1935.

Fred Feltham

More conventional working and with an almost new if somewhat grimy, 22xx having arrived at Winchester sometime in the late 1930's. Three engines of this type, Nos. 3210, 3211, and 3212, were sent new from Swindon to Didcot especially for DNS type workings in 1938 and replaced then certain tasks formally undertaken by the various 4-4-0's.

WORKING AT WINCHESTER Circa 1925

Before 7.00 am GW loco draws empty coaching stock into the up platform and waits.

2. At 7.00 am GW loco emerges from tunnel with down Bordesley Beer train and runs through to yard.

3. At 7.05 am GW loco leaves with up passenger train.

4. At 7.27 am GW loco emerges from tunnel with down goods and runs through to the yard.

5. Before 8.08 am GW loco runs light from yard into down platform and waits.

6. At 8.08 am SR loco arrives with up passenger train including through vehicles for Glasgow. Formation probably 2 x GWR, 2 x LNER and a 4-wheel van.

7. SR loco uncouples and runs forward into tunnel, GW loco runs forward from down platform into the tunnel behind it, then backs onto the up train. SR loco backs out of the tunnel into the down platform.

8. At 8.16 am GW loco leaves with up passenger service - 4 coaches and van.

9. SR loco runs back across points and waits either in horse dock or up platform.

10. At 8.28 am second SR loco brings goods from Eastleigh into goods yard - believed accessed direct from lower end. May become involved in some shunting but then departs light to Eastleigh at 8.40 am.

11. At 8.51 am GW loco arrives with down passenger train of three GWR coaches. Loco uncouples and runs forward into yard. SR loco

12. At 8.58 am SR loco departs for Shawford Junction with passenger train.

13. Before 10.12 am GW loco runs from yard into up platform and waits.

14. At 10.12 am GW loco emerges from tunnel with down mixed train comprising three GWR coaches with wagons and brake van behind. Wagons and brake van are uncoupled.

15. GW loco in up platform runs forward into tunnel then backs into down platform behind brake van but does not couple to van.

16. At 10.19 SR loco arrives with up passenger train comprising four GWR coaches. SR loco uncouples and runs forward into tunnel. GW loco runs into tunnel behind it then backs onto waiting up train.

17. SR loco backs into down platform behind brake van and wagons and couples to these.

18. 10.23 am. GW loco leaves with down passenger train for Shawford Junction.

19. 10.25 am GW loco leaves with up passenger train of four coaches.

20. SR loco propels wagons and brake van from down platform to Bar End yard - may do some shunting.

21. At 12.04 pm GW loco previously used at '18' returns with up passenger train comprising up to three GWR coaches, one 'six-wheeler' amd a four-wheeled van. Leaves for Didcot at 12.08 pm.

22. At 12.10 pm SR loco referred to at '16, 17 & 20', leaves down end of yard (?) with goods for Eastleigh. Certain of this traffic had arrived at 7.27 am - see '4'.

23. At 12.21 pm GW loco arrives on down goods train from Reading and runs into yard.

24. At about 1.20 pm GW loco leaves with up goods for Didcot.

25. At 1.24 pm GW loco arrives with down passenger train of two GWR coaces. Leaves for Shawford Junction at 1.27 pm.

26. At 2.28 pm GW loco previously referred to at '25' arrives back with up passenger. This was brought from Southampton as far as Eastleigh by the SR engine referred to at '22'. (According to George's notes the actual train in question comprised of no less 12 bogie coaches and an SR horsebox. This would certainly be unusual and no reason is given.) Leaves at 2.31 pm.

27. At 3.05 pm GW loco arrives with down passenger train of four coaches. Departs for Shawford Junction.

28. At 5.26 pm GW loco from '27' arrives back with up passenger train of four GWR coaches.

29. At 5.34 pm SR loco arrives light engine and runs into up platform.

30. At 5.40 pm GW loco emerges from tunnel with down passenger of two GWR coaches. Loco uncouples and runs forward into yard.

31. SR loco runs acrosss points and backs onto train of two GWR coaches. Leaves at 5.45 pm.

32. At 6.30 pm GW loco leaves goods yard and runs through platform with up goods to Reading. (This loco is likely to have been a Reading engine having previously arrived at '23'.

33. At 8.00 pm SR loco arrives with up passenger train of four GWR coaches. It runs around the train and waits in either the loading dock or behind the train in the up platform.

34. At 8.15 pm GW loco emerges from the tunnel with down passenger train of three GWR coaches, uncouples and runs forward to Bar End.

Opposite page; The DNS in 1936, and with Duke Class 4-4- No. 3267, 'Cornishman' entering the station on one of the through GWR engine workings over the DNS from Southampton.

C.R.L. Coles.

35. Immediately after this SR loco from '33' runs forward and then attaches to down train. Leaves for Shawford Junction at 8.25 pm.

36. Before 8.50 pm GW loco runs from yard along the down platform and into the tunnel. Then backs onto the four coaches waiting in the up platform. At 8.50. pm it leaves for Newbury. (This was a Saturday only working.)

37. At 11.20 pm GW loco - probably that previously used at No. 36, emerges from the tunnel with the return train from Newbury. After passengers have alighted the loco draws the empty coaches to Bar end and returns to shed. (Again a Saturday only working. Not surprisingly this late evening service was known as 'The Boozer'.)

Regular locomotives known to have been used by the GWR and SR around this time include from the SR, No. 6, and 'T1 class No. 367E'. Further engines of the same type, No. 8E and No. 362E . Visiting GWR locos known of include 'Dean Goods' No. 2463, No. 3551, and No. 3214. The remaining engines used would be those based at Winchester.

Running with a R.O.D. tender-these were not popular with the firemen, another 22xx passes the loading dock in the last years of peace. The loading dock would sometimes be used by Southern engines in the lay over between trains, although obviously they could not do this if another service was due to deposit or collect a horse box.

C.R.L. Coles.